Jean Aitchison is an independent consultant in library and information systems, specialising in thesaurus design and construction. Prior to taking up consultancy work, she held a number of posts in public and special libraries, including six years as head of a large industrial library and information service. She is the compiler, or co-compiler, of major thesauri, such as the *UNESCO thesaurus*, the *DHSS-DATA thesaurus*, the *Thesaurus on youth*, and the pioneering *Thesaurofacet*. She was also adviser on the design of the BSI *ROOT thesaurus*. She received the 1982 Ranganathan Award for her work on thesaurus development and the reconciliation of classification systems and thesauri.

Alan Gilchrist is a senior partner of Alan Gilchrist & Partners, a consultancy service concerned with information management and all aspects of information systems design and implementation. He is a Fellow of the Institute of Information Scientists and Editor-In-Chief of the *Journal of Information Science*. His publications include *The thesaurus in retrieval* (also published by Aslib) and he teaches, with Jean Aitchison, on the Aslib Thesaurus Construction course.

Thesaurus construction
A practical manual

Jean Aitchison

Alan Gilchrist

Second edition

Published by Aslib, The Association for Information Management,
26 –27 Boswell Street, London WC1N 3JZ

The publishers would like to thank those individuals and organizations
cited on pages 165 – 166 for permission to reproduce copyright material.

First published 1972
Second edition 1987

British Library Cataloguing in Publication Data

Aitchison, Jean
    Thesaurus construction : a practical manual. — 2nd ed.
    1. Subject headings
    I. Title II. Gilchrist, Alan, *1932–*
    025.4′9   Z695

ISBN 0-85142-197-0

Phototypeset by Auckland Litho Limited, 5–25 Burr Road, London SW18 4SG
Printed and bound in Great Britain by Henry Ling Limited, at the Dorset Press,
Dorchester, Dorset

Contents

Section A   Introduction

The aim of this manual is to provide a practical, concise and handy guide to the construction of thesauri for use in information retrieval. The thesaurus, in the context of this manual, is a 'vocabulary of controlled indexing language, formally organized so that *a priori* relationships between concepts are made explicit', to be used in information retrieval systems, whether these are databases, or printed indexes or catalogues.

There are two problems to be faced in keeping a book on this topic as short as possible. First, a large amount of theoretical material has had to be omitted. For further reading and reference, readers are referred to the items in the bibliography at the end of the manual, and in particular to the second edition of *Vocabulary control for information retrieval*, by F. W. Lancaster (46). Second, lack of space dictated that not all possible construction techniques could be illustrated fully in Section J, which is a practical summary of the preceding theory. Consequently, there is a bias in that section to the use of faceted techniques. Few apologies are made for this decision, as experience over the intervening years since the first publication of this manual has tended to confirm that facet analysis is used intuitively by many of those who attempt to determine thesaurus structure and the consequent relationships.

Even when theoretical aspects and alternative examples of practical techniques are omitted, this second edition shows an increase in size. In the fourteen years since the first edition, knowledge of thesaurus construction has developed and undergone painstaking analysis and systemization, in the course of the production of detailed international and national standards on the subject. A manual on thesaurus construction must be specific enough to comment on, and illustrate, the points raised in these standards. This new edition has also to cover adequately the use of computer aids in thesaurus construction – a new field, which was in its infancy in 1972, but now requires an extended section. It also has to cover other new developments, such as the merging and integration of thesauri and the design of searching thesauri, which have emerged in connection with the use of thesauri in online information retrieval.

The first section after the introduction (Section B) is concerned with the planning and design of thesaurus systems. This addresses such problems as when it is necessary to construct a thesaurus; and if a thesaurus is needed, what type of thesaurus would be most effective in a given situation. The section on planning precedes one (Section C) on thesaurus construction standards, which are adhered to fairly closely throughout the remaining chapters of the manual. The next four sections (D–G) deal with the various features of the thesaurus: namely, vocabulary control; specificity and compound terms; structure: basic relationships and classification; and auxiliary retrieval devices. These are followed by a section (H) describing and illustrating a number of possible forms of thesaurus presentation. The next section (I) discusses different types of thesauri, including multilingual thesauri, merged vocabularies and searching thesauri. Section J is concerned with practical aspects of construction, from term collection to determining structure, organization of layout and the writing of the introduction. Maintenance and updating are treated in the following Section K. Section L deals with computer aids and Section M lists the main packages and bureau services available. The manual concludes with a bibliography which includes both further reading and thesauri referred to in the text.

This manual, though not claiming to be more than an introductory text, should nevertheless be an adequate guide to the competent compilation of most thesauri, particularly if used in conjunction with the standards with which it is closely aligned. In the remaining circumstances, it will provide enough of an introduction to a complex subject for the reader to approach the task with a better understanding of the inherent problems.

Section B   *Planning and design of thesauri*

Before starting work on the construction of a thesaurus, the information system it is intended to serve should be studied. This will establish whether a thesaurus is needed, and if it is, what form it should take to meet the requirements of the system.

B1. Is a thesaurus necessary? Natural versus controlled language

With the development of online information systems using free text (that is to say the natural language of words in the titles, abstracts, and full text of the documents) as a means of retrieval, the usefulness of controlled language (that is classification systems, subject headings, and thesauri) has to be reassessed. The role of the thesaurus is changing, but it is likely to remain as an important retrieval tool, though with some of its features modified.

In manual systems the usefulness of controlled language is undisputed, both in pre-coordinated systems such as card catalogues and printed indexes, and also in post-coordinate systems employing punched cards, using, for example, optical coincidence to correlate subjects mechanically. Manual systems are not capable of dealing with untreated natural language because of the large number of cards which would have to be manipulated to handle the words involved. The thesaurus is of use in computer-produced printed indexes to control synonyms and provide the basis of 'see also' references, although natural language title and title-enriched indexes with free-text assigned keywords are thesaurus-independent. In machine-readable post-coordinate systems, natural language is frequently the only retrieval language, but there are also databases which use controlled language alone. On the increase are databases using natural and controlled languages combined in two-level or hybrid systems. In Figure 1 the advantages and disadvantages of natural and controlled language are compared. Natural language has a number of advantages over controlled language but it also has weaknesses. Figure 1 indicates how controlled language may be used to compensate for the deficiencies of free text and vice versa in mixed controlled and natural language systems. The natural language gives currency and specificity to improve precision (the ability to exclude irrelevant information). Natural language's exhaustivity of coverage, where abstracts and full text are included, ensures good recall (the retrieval of relevant information in the database). On the other hand, the controlled language increases recall by synonym control and provision of an *aide-mémoire* to related terms. The controlled language may also improve precision by the use of compound terms, homograph control and devices such as 'links' and 'roles'. In some hybrid systems, the controlled language is simple, and non-specific, acting primarily as a

Figure 1. Comparison of natural and controlled language

Natural language

Strengths

○ High specificity gives precision. Excels in retrieving 'individual' terms – names of persons, organizations, etc.

○ Exhaustivity gives potential for high recall. Does not apply to title-only databases.

○ Up-to-date. New terms immediately available.

○ Words of author used – no misinterpretation by indexer.

○ Natural language words used by searcher.

○ Low input costs.

○ Easier exchange of material between databases – language incompatibility removed.

Weaknesses

○ Intellectual effort placed on searcher. Problems arise with terms having many synonyms and several species.

○ Syntax problems. Danger of false drops through incorrect term association.

○ Exhaustivity may lead to loss of precision.

Controlled language

Weaknesses

○ Lack of specificity, even in detailed systems.

○ Lack of exhaustivity. Cost of indexing to level of natural language prohibitive. Also terms may be omitted in error by indexers.

○ Not immediately up-to-date. Time lag while terms are added to thesaurus.

○ Words of author liable to be misconstrued. Errors in indexing terms can cause losses.

○ Artificial language has to be learned by the searcher.

○ High input costs.

○ Incompatibility a barrier to easy exchange.

Strengths

○ Eases the burden of searching:
  – controls synonyms and near-synonyms and leads specific natural language concepts to the nearest preferred terms to broaden search
  – qualifies homographs
  – provides scope notes
  – displays broader, narrower and related terms
  – expresses concepts elusive in free text.

○ Overcomes syntax problems with compound terms and other devices.

○ At normal levels of indexing, avoids precision loss through over-exhaustivity (i.e. retrieval of minor concepts of peripheral interest).

○ An asset in numerical databases and multilingual systems.

Both natural and controlled language systems offer the same powerful search aids – truncation, word proximity, etc.

recall-improving device, but in other systems, the controlled language is fairly specific and sophisticated, as in the *INSPEC* and *DHSS-DATA* databases which use a thesaurus and a classification system to complement the free-text terms and to improve recall and precision.

A thesaurus may still be necessary even if the expense of indexing becomes prohibitive in computerized systems. In this case, the thesaurus would be used only at the search stage, and would be named a post-controlled thesaurus, or a searching thesaurus (see I3). Natural language systems and the role of the controlled language are discussed in Lancaster (46, Chapter 17), Fugmann (33), Perez (56), Johnston (44), Snow (63), Sievert and Boyce (61), Markey and others (49), and Dubois (28).

Another future role for thesauri and classification systems is likely to be as contributory tools in the organization of the knowledge base in expert systems.

B2. Information system considerations

If it is decided that a thesaurus is to be constructed, the information system and database should be examined next in more detail to find what thesaurus characteristics would best serve the system and improve its performance.

B2.1. Subject field
Consideration should be given first to the subject field of the system. The boundaries of the field should be defined. Core areas where depth treatment is essential should be identified, and also marginal areas where more superficial treatment will be sufficient. In the central area, which is likely to include specialized knowledge, a new thesaurus may have to be constructed, whereas in the peripheral areas existing thesauri or parts of these may be used.

B2.2. Type of literature/data
Is the database to contain documents or factual, numerical data as in a databank? If it is the latter, a thesaurus linked with a classification or coding system might be the best choice. If the database is bibliographic, the type of literature which predominates should be considered. Is it mainly monograph literature, or do reports, journal articles, conference papers and other serial publications predominate? Books do not normally require the in-depth indexing of serials and this will have a bearing on the specificity of the thesaurus. (Where books do require in-depth indexing it is often sensible to treat sections or chapters as separate items.)

B2.3. Quantity of literature/data
The size of the file and the rate of growth should be noted. The larger the quantity of documents/data to be indexed the greater the input costs. This may be an influencing factor in deciding to opt for a searching thesaurus rather than one used for indexing. On the other hand the quantities to be handled might weigh in a decision to design a thesaurus with precision devices to avoid the retrieval of irrelevant

documents, admissible in a small file, but not tolerable in a large one. If the database is small and growing slowly, a detailed, extensive thesaurus could be an expensive luxury, unless the subject field covered is highly complex.

B2.4. Language considerations

Is the system bilingual or multilingual? If information is input and searched in more than one language a bilingual or multilingual thesaurus is needed, and the special construction problems this implies should be taken into consideration (see I1).

B2.5. System users

It is important to know who are the users of the system. Will the end-users operate the system or will they leave this to qualified intermediaries? If the system is end-user operated, the thesaurus should be user-friendly, having a minimum of complex devices, and using familiar uncomplicated terminology. The controlled language should be unobtrusive. As far as possible the natural language terms of the user should be mapped onto the nearest equivalent controlled terms to improve access and to allow for automatic translation of natural to controlled language in online searching.

B2.6. Questions, searches, profiles

What type of questions will be put to the system? Will they be general or detailed? If only broad subjects are treated, a specific vocabulary will be redundant, whereas if enquiries are for detailed information then the indexing terms must parallel this specificity. How many questions will be put to the system? Indexing may be uneconomic if searching is infrequent, and a thesaurus designed as a searching tool for a natural language system may be preferred. On the other hand, a sophisticated thesaurus for indexing and searching may be justified in a heavily used system, handling detailed questions, to improve the speed and quality of searches. A thesaurus will also be of great benefit in alerting systems, where profiles of the interests of individuals or groups are automatically matched against periodic input.

B2.7. Resources available

○ Financial resources

This is a key factor, although often outside the control of the information system. The type and size of the organization, whether it is an international body, government establishment or an academic, institutional, commercial or industrial organization will have some influence on the finances available. Industrial organizations are particularly susceptible to financial fluctuations, but all information projects, not excluding those which are government-sponsored, are liable to cut-backs. Where resources are limited or subequently curtailed, economies may have to be made in the thesaurus project. This might take the form of adapting a thesaurus used by another organization, rather than developing a new one. If a new thesaurus has to be compiled, costs can be cut if the size is reduced, specificity moderated and structure simplified.

○ Staff resources

If there is a shortage of staff to operate the system, the thesaurus should be designed to be easily maintained. This implies that it should be of moderate size and specificity. The thesaurus should be as user-friendly as possible, so that the end-user may search the system without help.

○ What type of equipment is available?
With the continuing reduction in computer costs and the increasing availability of microcomputers, even small thesauri of a few thousand terms may be mechanized. The selection of software for thesaurus handling (see Section M) is improving all the time, so that lack of software should not restrict the choice of thesaurus layout, or its use as an integral part of a computerized information system.

B3. Choice of thesaurus

Once the information system parameters are established it is time to concentrate attention on the type of thesaurus which will best serve the system.

B3.1. New thesaurus versus adaptation

There are several published bibliographies of thesauri (8, 22, 29, 47), including one in a 1979 edition of *Aslib Proceedings* (35), giving details of the Aslib Library thesaurus collection. This list was updated in the March and September issues of *Aslib Information* (7) until 1983 and since then in the *Current Awareness Bulletin*, March and September issues (21). Aslib also holds information on thesauri and classification systems under construction. *Online Notes* (54), issued monthly by Aslib's Information Resources Centre, also reports the publication of new thesauri. Information on new thesauri, subject heading lists and classification systems in languages other than English is issued regularly in the *Bibliographic Bulletin* of the Clearinghouse at the Polish Institute for Scientific, Technical and Economic Information (IINTE) (41) – see also J14. An important bibliography of current thesauri which have appeared in at least one of the official languages of the European Communities is prepared and updated by the Gesellschaft für Information und Dokumentation (GID) (34). This database is also available on ECHO, a service operated by the Commission of the European Communities.

The likely indexing languages should be examined to see if they may be (a) adopted *in toto*, with minimum alteration, or (b) adopted as an acceptable framework, within which certain areas must be modified or developed in greater detail.

If neither of these courses is appropriate (as suitable indexing languages are non-existent), it will be necessary to construct a purpose-built thesaurus with a system-oriented framework. Even so, existing thesauri should not be overlooked, since they may contain sections suitable for extraction, amendment and use in the new system.

These sections might be commonly applicable schedules dealing with materials, physical properties, and geographical divisions, or more specialized sections of marginal subject interest, which might be accepted into the new thesaurus with little alteration. It is usual to acknowledge all sources used in this way in the introduction to the thesaurus.

B3.2. Thesaurus design elements

An indexing language consists not only of indexing terms or 'vocabulary', but also of certain 'indexing language devices', which were first analysed by the Cranfield Project (17), and which, when varied, will influence the thesaurus performance. These devices should be carefully selected, bearing in mind the effect they may have on retrieval. Indexing language devices fall into two groups: those which tend to improve the retrieval of relevant documents – 'recall devices'; and those which tend to prevent the recall of irrelevant information – 'precision devices'. Some devices may improve both recall and precision, for example the display of structural relationships. Detailed consideration is given to these devices later in this manual (Sections D–G) but a summary is presented below.

Recall devices include:

○ Control of word form (number, grammatical form, word order and other variants)
This device prevents the loss of relevant information through the scatter of concepts under different forms of the same term (see D2–D4).

○ Word fragment searching
This device is not an integral part of the thesaurus, but is used in online searching, whatever the type of indexing language, to achieve the same result as word form control, and in addition provides for improved recall by broadening the search to include word stems and other fragments of words. For example, using right truncation 'Hous*' will retrieve Housing, Houses, Housebound, etc., and left truncation '*molecular' will retrieve Intramolecular and Intermolecular (see G2.2).

○ Control of synonyms and quasi-synonyms
This device prevents the scattering of synonyms and quasi-synonyms across the database, by referring non-preferred synonyms to the preferred term (see F1.1–F1.2).

○ Specific to general entry terms
This device improves recall by leading the searcher from specific concepts, too detailed for the thesaurus, to the nearest indexing term available to represent them (see F1.3).

○ Structural relationships, hierarchical and non-hierarchical relationships
This device improves recall, widening a search by the introduction of closely related classes (see F2–F6). It may also improve precision, by suggesting narrower, more specific terms.

Precision devices include:

○ Specificity of the indexing language
The greater the detail and number of terms, the more precisely may the subject of the documents be described. Specificity controls the precision capabilities of the system and demands greater skill in indexing and searching (see E1).

○ Coordination
A most powerful precision device. By increasing the number of terms in combination in indexing or in searching, the concepts required will be defined more accurately and unwanted information eliminated. Recall is improved by reversing the process and reducing the combination level (see G1).

○ Compound terms – level of term pre-coordination
This is another form of coordination, but one built into the thesaurus, rather than being a feature of the operational system. Compound terms ensure that the subject of a document may be minutely identified, preventing the retrieval of non-relevant documents (see E2).

○ Homographs and scope notes
These restrict and clarify the meaning of otherwise ambiguous terms, resulting in more precise terms for retrieval (see D5).

○ Word distance indication
An online searching device to improve precision by specifying that words should be adjacent, or within the same sentence or paragraph (see G2.3).

○ Structural relationships
These may lead the indexer or searcher from broad concepts to more specific terms, which will narrow the search and tend to exclude unwanted information.

○ Links and roles
Devices which overcome false coordination and incorrect relationships, by labelling groups of associated terms or indicating the roles of terms (see G3–G4).

○ Treatment and other aspect codes (see G5)

○ Weighting
A device for differentiating between major and minor concepts (see G6).

Some devices, including specificity, hierarchies and synonym control can be regarded as an integral part of the vocabulary. Other devices, such as coordination, or weighting, operate independently of the vocabulary and can be called 'auxiliary devices' (see Section G). Other thesaurus-independent devices include online word fragment searching and word distance indication.

In broad terms, there is an inverse relationship between recall and precision, which suggests that a gain in recall is accompanied by a loss in precision, and a gain in precision by a recall loss. When designing a thesaurus, it should be remembered that the introduction of a precision device, such as high specificity and multiword terms, will lower recall performance; whereas reducing vocabulary specificity, using single word terms or excluding auxiliary precision devices, will improve recall but impair precision.

The interaction between controlled and natural language has already been discussed (see B1). The reciprocal advantages of the combination of the two systems is another factor to bear in mind in thesaurus design. Natural language can compensate for lack of specificity in the controlled language, and improve precision; while controlled language can improve the recall through its control of synonyms and near-synonyms, and display of relationships. Also, the precision devices of controlled language, such as compound terms and homograph qualification, may offset the precision loss in exhaustive natural language systems.

A complex thesaurus, highly structured, with a systematic display, specific terminology and compound terms will be expensive to construct and to operate at the input stage, and will require effort to maintain. The cost of this effort should be balanced against the expected improvement in performance. On the other hand, thesauri which are cheap to produce and maintain, having broad terminology and minimum structure, may be more difficult, and therefore more expensive, to operate successfully at the search stage. If a broad thesaurus is used to improve recall in combination with natural language, supplying detailed terminology, precision may be improved without heavy expenditure on thesaurus development (46, Chapter 18).

Section C

Thesaurus construction and development standards

Thesaurus construction and development standards and guidelines are essential documents for thesaurus compilers. They should be read and absorbed before the work commences and always be available for reference during the operation.

Standards exist for both monolingual and multilingual thesauri. For monolingual thesauri the International Standard is ISO 2788 issued by the International Organization for Standardization. It was first published in 1974. A second edition was accepted in 1985 and published in 1986 (42).

In the new edition of ISO 2788, the alphabetical approach represented by the American *Thesaurus of engineering and scientific terms* (*TEST*) of 1967, and the classificatory approach of European compilers are combined in the same Standard. (See 46, Chapter 5). National standards for monolingual thesauri include the British Standard 5723 (14) and the American Standard ANSI Z39.19 (6), the French Standard AFNOR NFZ 47–100 (9) and the German Standard DIN 1463 (24).

The International Standard on multilingual thesauri is ISO 5964 accepted in 1985 (43). The British equivalent is British Standard 6723:1985 (15).

The rules referred to in the sections which follow in this manual are based on the latest edition of ISO 2788 for monolingual thesauri and ISO 5964 for multilingual thesauri, and their British Standard exact equivalents BS 5723 and BS 6723.

Section D

Vocabulary control

Control of terminology in a thesaurus is achieved in various ways. First, the form of the term is controlled, whether this involves grammatical form, spelling, singular and plural form, abbreviations or compound form of the term. Second, a choice is made between two or more synonyms or quasi-synonyms available to express the same concept. Third, a decision is made on whether to admit proper nouns, and in what form. Fourth, the meaning of the term, which in a dictionary might be accompanied by illustrations of different usage, is deliberately restricted to that most effective for the purposes of a particular thesaurus. The restriction is indicated in a thesaurus by the addition of scope notes and definitions, and qualifying phrases in the case of homographs. All these methods of thesaurus control are dealt with in this section, except for compound terms which are considered in Section E. Synonyms and quasi-synonyms, although mentioned here under choice of term, are dealt with more fully in F1.

D1. Indexing terms – preferred and non-preferred

As defined by ISO 2788, an indexing term is 'the representation of a concept'. It can consist of more than one word, and is then known as a compound term. In a controlled language an indexing term may be either a preferred term or a non-preferred term. The preferred term is 'a term used consistently when indexing to represent a given concept'. It is sometimes known as a 'descriptor' or 'keyword'. A non-preferred term is the 'synonym or quasi-synonym of a preferred term'. It is not used in indexing, but provides a 'lead-in' or entry point from which the user may be directed by the instruction USE to the appropriate preferred term. The non-preferred term is also known as a 'non-descriptor'.

D2. Indexing terms – basic types

Indexing terms can be divided into basic types, according to the fundamental categories used in the technique of facet analysis, described in F4 below. Two main categories and their sub-divisions are set out in ISO 2788, these being concrete entities and abstract concepts.

Examples:

Concrete entities

Things and their physical parts
PRIMATES
HEAD
BUILDINGS
FLOORS

Materials
CEMENT
WOOD
ALUMINIUM

Abstract concepts

Actions and events
EVOLUTION
SKATING
MANAGEMENT

Abstract entities, and properties of things, materials and actions
LAW
THEORY
STRENGTH
EFFICIENCY

Disciplines and sciences
PHYSICS
METEOROLOGY
PSYCHOLOGY

etc.

These basic classes have importance in deciding whether the singular or plural form is to be used and in determining the validity of hierarchical relationships, as well as in the analysis of subject fields.

D3. Indexing terms – form of term

An obvious step in vocabulary control is to regulate the form of admissible indexing terms. This section considers acceptable grammatical forms, singular and plural forms, variable spellings, and transliteration. Abbreviated forms and acronyms are dealt with in F1 under equivalence relationships. Terms in compound form are treated in E2.

D3.1. Nouns, adjectives, adverbs, verbs

○ Nouns and noun phrases
Indexing terms usually consist of nouns and noun phrases. The most common form of noun phrase is the adjectival phrase.

Example:

WOMEN WORKERS

The less common, but still admissible, form is the prepositional phrase.

Example:

PHILOSOPHY OF EDUCATION

○ Adjectives
According to the standards, adjectives are not generally acceptable as indexing terms, although some thesauri contain a limited number of generally applicable adjectives, relating to time, conditions, size, shape, position and the like.

Examples:

SIMULTANEOUS
MINIATURE
VARIABLE
AUXILIARY
PORTABLE
AXIAL
RECTANGULAR

These are used in post-coordinate systems to represent adjectival components of compound terms to be combined with appropriate nouns.

Example:

Portable typewriters
USE TYPEWRITERS and PORTABLE

This use of adjectives is not mentioned in ISO 2788. It may be deduced, however, that it would not be favoured, as most of the compound terms which are factored by this use of adjectives are recommended by the standards to be retained in compound form, since they are mainly entities and actions qualified by their properties (see E2). If it is necessary to include these general concepts in the thesaurus, whether to be used alone or as part of a factored compound term, they should be given in the noun form.

Examples:

MINIATURE SIZE
PORTABLE DEVICES
AXIAL POSITION
TRIANGULAR SHAPE

○ Adverbs
Adverbs such as 'very' and 'highly' are excluded from thesauri, unless they form part of a compound term.

Example:

VERY LARGE SCALE INTEGRATION

○ Verbs
Verbs in the infinitive or participle form are also excluded. Nouns and verbal nouns are used to represent them in thesauri.

Examples:

COMMUNICATION (*not* Communicate)
ADMINISTRATION (*not* Administer)

D3.2. Singular and plural forms
In languages where the distinction between singular and plural forms can be made, compilers are influenced by the traditions of their own language communities. Those working in the French and German languages, for example, tend to prefer the singular, with a limited number of exceptions, such as where the singular and plural forms have different meanings. In English-speaking communities, terms may be expressed in either the singular or the plural, determined by rules set out in the Standards, which are considered in this section.

When deciding upon the use of singular or plural forms in the English language, it is useful to divide terms into the two basic categories of concrete entities and abstract concepts, described in D2.

○ Concrete entities
These include 'count nouns' and 'non-count nouns'.

Count nouns are defined as 'names of countable objects that are subject to the question "How many?" but not "How much?"' and are given as plurals.

Examples:

PLANETS
ESTUARIES
PLOUGHS
CHILDREN
AQUARIA

The rules are modified in the case of parts of the body. Plurals are used when more than one part occurs in a 'fully formed organism', but if only one is present the singular is preferred.

Examples:

EYES	*but*	MOUTH
ARMS		RESPIRATORY SYSTEM

Non-count nouns are defined as 'names of materials or substances which are subject to the question "How much?" but not "How many?"', and are expressed as singulars.

Examples:

NICKEL
MICA
SNOW
FLOUR
LACE

This rule is more flexible, and consequently more ambiguous, than the 'count nouns' rule, since it allows exceptions in cases when 'the community of users served by the index regards a given substance or material as a class with more than one member. The class should then be expressed in the plural'.

Examples:

STEELS
FRUITS
CEMENTS

○ Abstract concepts
Abstract concepts, comprising abstract entities and phenomena, properties, systems of belief, activities and disciplines are shown in the singular form.

Examples:

Abstract entities and phenomena

AUTHORITY
LOGIC
SOCIAL DISTANCE

Properties

PHOTOCONDUCTIVITY
HARDENABILITY
ECCENTRICITY
EMOTIONAL INSTABILITY

Systems of belief

SOCIALISM
HINDUISM

Activities

EXPLORATION
FUSION
PACKAGING
CONFLICT

Disciplines

BIOCHEMISTRY
ENGINEERING
ETHNOLOGY

As for non-count concrete entities, if an abstract concept is regarded as 'a class with more than one member', the term representing that class is expressed in the plural.

Examples:

BIOLOGICAL SCIENCES
IDEOLOGIES
EMOTIONS

○ Exceptions

Occasionally, the singular and plural of the same word will have different meanings. When this occurs, both terms are entered in the thesaurus. If necessary, the distinction should be shown either by adding a qualifying term or phrase to both terms, or by changing one of the terms into a compound term.

Example:

COATING (material)   COATINGS
                    or
COATING (process)   COATING PROCESS

Entry points are not normally given in the thesaurus from the non-preferred to the preferred singular or plural form. An exception is made when the difference in spelling separates the two forms of the term in the alphabetical sequence.

Example:

Foot
USE FEET

D3.3. Spelling

Spelling should conform to a recognized dictionary or glossary, and/or to the house style of the organization responsible for the thesaurus. In any case, the most acceptable spelling for the intended users of the thesaurus should be adopted. This rule extends to the choice between spellings made for cultural reasons, for example, between English English and American English. In thesauri originating in the United Kingdom, English English should be used, consistently, with a note in the introduction stating this policy. Reference should be made from commonly recognized variant spellings to the preferred forms. This rule applies also to references from American-English spellings to English English in thesauri using English English, when the thesaurus is likely to be used extensively by American-English language communities. Examples of references between terms with different spellings are given in F1.

D3.4. Transliteration
To ensure consistency in transliterating terms from languages with different alphabets, the relevant ISO standard should be consulted and followed as far as possible.

D3.5. Punctuation
Punctuation marks are kept to a minimum. Apostrophes, for example, are omitted. Parentheses, however, should be used to enclose qualifying expressions, which are included as part of the term, to prevent ambiguity (see Homographs, D5.1). Commas are used in non-preferred, indirect entries leading to direct-form compound terms, except where parentheses are used for this purpose (see E2).

D3.5.1. Hyphens
Hyphens in compound terms are avoided where possible, either by leaving a space or by dropping the space between the words. Spaces may be dropped in the case of prefixes, which may be attached to base words.

Examples:

MULTIETHNIC SOCIETY
NONMETALS
POSTGRADUATE COURSES

The hyphen should be retained when the separate words must be preserved, and where the lack of a hyphen would result in ambiguities. Hyphens should also be retained in letter-word combinations.

Examples:

COPPER-CONTAINING ALLOYS
PARENT-TEACHER RELATIONSHIP
DRAW-OFF TAPS
PROTON-DEUTERON INTERACTION
N-TYPE STARS

ISO 2788 does not make recommendations on punctuation, so that the house style of the organization responsible for the individual thesaurus may be the influencing factor regarding hyphens. This results in differences in practice, particularly in the treatment of prefixes in English-language thesauri. For rules for filing terms containing hyphens, see H1.4.

D4. Indexing terms – choice of term

In this section, various types of terms and choices between them are considered. These include loan words, slang, popular terms, trade names, and proper names. Further detail on choice between terms is given in F1, which deals with synonyms and quasi-synonyms.

D4.1. Loan words

Well-established words from other languages may be admitted to the thesaurus. If a translation exists, but is not frequently used, it should be treated as a non-preferred term, and a reciprocal reference made between it and the loan word with the prefixes UF (use for) and USE.

Example:

WELTSCHMERZ
UF World weariness

World weariness USE WELTSCHMERZ

Should the translation or nearest equivalent term become more frequently used than the loan word, the loan word should be relegated to the status of a non-preferred term.

Example:

SOCIO-CULTURAL ANIMATION
UF Animation socio-culturelle

Animation socio-culturelle USE SOCIO-CULTURAL ANIMATION

D4.2. Common names and trade names

The Standards recommend that common names should be preferred to trade names, where a suitable common term exists. The trade name should be admitted as a non-preferred term only if it is likely to be sought by the user. Examples of common and trade names are given in F1.

D4.3. Popular names and scientific names

Where there is a choice between popular and scientific names, it is the advice of the Standards to choose the form most likely to be sought by the users of the thesaurus. In a thesaurus for a medical community the term RUBELLA might be used, whereas in a general or social welfare thesaurus, the popular form GERMAN MEASLES might be preferred. Reciprocal references should be made between the two forms of the term. Further examples of popular and scientific terms are given in F1.

D4.4. Place names

Where there is more than one form of a place name in a single language, for example 'official' and 'popular' or original and vernacular, ISO 2788 recommends that the one most familiar to the users of the thesaurus should be chosen as the preferred term. If both are equally familiar, preference should be given to the 'official' or original version.

Example:

FEDERAL REPUBLIC OF GERMANY
  UF West Germany

West Germany USE FEDERAL REPUBLIC OF GERMANY

D4.5. Identifiers: proper names of institutions, persons, etc.

Although names of institutions, persons, processes, types of equipment, etc. are important access points for the retrieval of information, they are often excluded from the thesaurus or, alternatively, their numbers are limited. Identifiers, in some systems, may be held in a separate file, which controls the form of the proper name, as for standard cataloguing practice, but gives no structural relationships. Geographic names are sometimes treated as identifiers. ISO 2788 gives the following rules for the form of proper names.

a.   Names of national and local institutions, which conduct their business (including publishing) in one language, should be entered in their untranslated forms. A reference from the translated form should be made if it exists.

Example:

CENTRO DE DOCUMENTACÂO CIENTIFICA
   UF Centre for Scientific Documentation (Lisbon)

Centre for Scientific Documentation (Lisbon)
   USE CENTRO DE DOCUMENTACÂO CIENTIFICA

b.   Names of international organizations, or local organizations which publish documents in more than one language, should be given in the most familiar form to the users of the thesaurus, with references from other forms, if the thesaurus is likely to be used by members of other language communities.

Example:

INTERNATIONAL FEDERATION FOR
   DOCUMENTATION
   UF Fédération International de Documentation

Fédération International de Documentation
   USE INTERNATIONAL FEDERATION OF
   DOCUMENTATION

c.   Personal names should be given in their original forms, unless the local form of name, notably of historical figures who have achieved international recognition, is better known to the users of the thesaurus. In this case the local name is preferred and a reference made from the original form.

Example (in an English-language thesaurus):

HENRY OF NAVARRE
   UF Henri de Navarre

Henri de Navarre
   USE HENRY OF NAVARRE

D5. Indexing terms – restriction and clarification of meaning

D5.1. Homographs and homonyms

Homographs are words having the same spelling as another but different in origin and meaning.

Example:

CELLS

which may refer to biological microsystems or electrical equipment.

Homographs may also have different pronunciations.

Example:

READING

which may refer to a communication process or to the town in England.

Homographs are sometimes referred to as polysemes, 'of many meanings', or as homonyms. Homonyms may be defined broadly as 'the same word used to denote different things', or more narrowly as 'words having the same sound but different meanings', that is, only one possible pronunciation (see Cells above).

The usual method of removing ambiguities caused by homographs is to add qualifiers (sometimes printed within parentheses) after the terms, to distinguish the two or more different meanings.

Examples:

CELLS (biology)
CELLS (electric)

READING (place)
READING (process)

The qualifier becomes an integral part of the term. An alternative method, possible in some cases, is to represent one or both of the meanings by a compound term in the direct form.

Example:

CELLS (or BIOLOGICAL CELLS)

ELECTRIC CELLS

An entry point should be made from the word Cells in the compound term to the full term.

Example:

Cells, electric
    USE ELECTRIC CELLS

D5.2. Scope notes (SNs) and definitions

As a general rule, complete definitions, as found in a dictionary, are not given in a thesaurus, but limited definitions, and even expanded definitions, are sometimes needed to supplement the meaning conveyed by the thesaurus structure. Definitions tend to be necessary most frequently in social science, humanities and the arts thesauri, to clarify imprecise terminology, which occurs more often in these subject areas.

Examples:

CULTURAL MODELS

  SN Systems of relations providing specific arrangements for each particular culture and regulating for each individual member the behaviour he must have in order to function as a member of his group.

SEGREGATION

    SN   Involuntary or voluntary concentration of particular groups (especially ethnic groups) in particular areas, or restriction of access of such groups to particular facilities or opportunities.

The source of the definition may be added, in parentheses, at the end of the definition. A code may be used to represent the source, and full details of the source should be given in the thesaurus introduction.

The scope note, as opposed to the limited definition, is used in the thesaurus in several ways. It may be used to indicate restrictions placed on the meaning of an indexing term.

Example:

INCOME

    SN   Income of individual organization or person.
           Otherwise use National Income.

It may be used to specify the range of topics covered by a concept for which only the generic term is included in the thesaurus. This occurs in marginal fields, or in thesauri covering a wide range of subjects at a limited depth.

Example:

INTEGRATED CIRCUIT TECHNOLOGY

    SN   Includes substrates, epitaxial layers, photoprocessing and microassembly.

The scope note may also serve to convey instructions to indexers on how indexing terms should be used, especially regarding the treatment of compound terms.

Example:

INTERIOR LIGHTING

    SN   For lighting of specific buildings or spaces combine with appropriate terms, e.g. Shop lighting use Shops and Interior lighting.

The scope note is also used to indicate 'dummy terms', that is terms needed to elucidate the structure of a systematic display (see H3), but which are themselves unsuitable for indexing. This would be followed by a class mark.

Example:

EDUCATION OF SPECIFIC CATEGORIES OF STUDENTS **BV**

    SN   Do not use as an indexing term
    NT   Exceptional student education
           Parent education
           Womens education

The scope note may also provide term histories, indicating, for example, when a term was adopted, or when changes in the scope of a term took place:

Example:

TRANSIT TIME NOISE
   SN   Invalid term. After 1981 Random noise used.

A scope note or definition is not regarded as forming part of the term to which it refers, as is the case with the qualifier attached to a homograph.

Section E   *Specificity and compound terms*

E1. Vocabulary specificity

The specificity of a retrieval language vocabulary depends on the ability of the indexing terms to express the subject in depth and in detail. Specificity has an important influence on the performance of the language, as it determines the accuracy with which concepts may be defined and consequently the facility to exclude unwanted documents.

In Figure 2 the specificity increases from indexing language A to indexing language D. In system A the concept Brown bread will be indexed by the term Food, and in B by Bakery products, in system C by Bread and in D by the identical term Brown bread. If a lead-in is included in the entry vocabulary to the broader term under which the term is subsumed in A, B and C, there is an equal chance of recalling documents indexed on these topics in all four systems.

However, all four systems do not perform equally well in excluding unwanted material. In system A, Brown bread will be recalled with all documents referring to Food; in system B with all documents on Bakery products; and in system C with documents on all types of Bread. Only in system D will no irrelevant documents be recalled (except for those which may have been incorrectly indexed). With a good entry vocabulary, recall performance is not affected by specificity of the language, although precision is.

Figure 2. Vocabulary specificity

Indexing language A	Indexing language B	Indexing language C	Indexing language D

Food	Food
	  Bakery Products
		Food
		  Bakery Products
		    Bread
			Food
			  Bakery Products
			    Bread
			      (By form)
			      Bread Loaves
			      Bread Rolls
			      (By ingredient)
			  → Brown Bread
			      White Bread
			      Starch Reduced Bread

System A – Brown Bread, USE Food
System B – Brown Bread, USE Bakery Products
System C – Brown Bread, USE Bread
System D – Brown Bread

The disadvantage of a highly specific vocabulary is that the number of indexing terms is increased, and it is consequently more expensive to compile, maintain, and operate. To construct a specific vocabulary, subject fields must be described accurately, which calls for greater knowledge of the terms, their meanings and relationships. The problems of term selection, organization and display are multiplied. Changes are needed more frequently in a specific vocabulary than in a system using only the more static broader concepts as indexing terms.

To reduce effort and expense, specificity may by dropped to a lower level, and recall will not be lost if lead-in entries are made from the specific concepts to the broader term or terms in combination used to represent them. As is illustrated in Figure 2 there are varying levels of specificity which may be chosen. In the same system different levels of specificity will be appropriate: a high level of specificity for areas central to the subject field and lower levels in the intermediate and marginal areas.

E2. Compound terms: levels of pre-coordination

According to the International Standard ISO 2788: 'it is a general rule that terms in a thesaurus should represent simple or unitary concepts as far as possible, and compound terms should be factored (i.e. split) into simple elements, except when this is likely to affect the users' understanding'. In a thesaurus, 'complex subjects should be expressed by the combination of separate terms and these may be assigned as independent search keys in a post-coordinate system, or they may function as components of pre-coordinated index entries'.

Example:

The phrase
Workload of dentists in Scotland
factors into
WORKLOAD + DENTISTS + SCOTLAND

A difficult and constantly occurring problem in thesaurus construction is knowing when to factor compound terms into simpler terms and when it may be better for system performance to retain the compound term (also known as the pre-coordinated term). A thesaurus having a majority of single terms is said to have a low pre-coordination level, and one with many two- or three-word compound terms is said to have a high pre-coordination level.

E2.1. Structure of compound terms
A compound term may be either an *adjectival phrase*, such as DRIED VEGETABLES or a *prepositional phrase*, such as PHILOSOPHY OF EDUCATION.

A compound term may be analysed into two parts: the focus and the difference.

○ The focus
This is the noun component, also known as the genus term or the head, which, in the words of ISO 2788, identifies the broader class of things or events to which the term as a whole refers.

Examples:

VEGETABLES
in the adjectival phrase DRIED VEGETABLES

PHILOSOPHY
in the prepositional phrase PHILOSOPHY OF EDUCATION

In a one-word term such as VEGETABLES or PHILOSOPHY the word *is* the focus.

○ The difference
This is the part of the compound term, also known as the modifier or species term, which refers to a characteristic, or a logical difference, which when applied to a focus, narrows its connotation and so specifies one of its subclasses.

Examples:

DRIED
which specifies a subclass of vegetables in DRIED VEGETABLES

OF EDUCATION
which specifies a subclass of philosophy in PHILOSOPHY OF EDUCATION

E2.2. Order of words in compound terms
Natural language order (also known as direct form) should be used to enter compound terms in a thesaurus.

Examples:

DRIED VEGETABLES, not VEGETABLES, DRIED

PHILOSOPHY OF EDUCATION, not EDUCATION, PHILOSOPHY OF
(note, the adjectival phrase Educational philosophy is acceptable)

WATER SOURCES, not SOURCES, WATER

Reciprocal entries should always be made from the indirect form of the prepositional phrase, but in the case of the adjectival phrase, only if the focal noun, for example 'sources' in 'Water sources', does not appear as an indexing term in the thesaurus.

Examples:

Education, philosophy of, USE PHILOSOPHY OF EDUCATION

Sources, water, USE WATER SOURCES

E2.3. Effect of compound terms on performance
The pre-coordination level of terms in a thesaurus is directly related to the specificity of the vocabulary. The more complex the indexing terms, the more specific the vocabulary and the greater the total number of terms. One of the factors which affect the pre-coordination level is the generality of the subject field. In a thesaurus covering a limited field, terms may be used without qualification to represent concepts which may be ambiguous in a wider context. For example, in a thesaurus devoted to Education, the single terms *Buildings*, *Testing* may be unequivocal, whereas in a general thesaurus having specific terms for other applications of these concepts, such as *Public Buildings*, *Mechanical Testing*, the compound terms *Educational Buildings* and

Educational Testing would be needed to distinguish the educational from these other aspects.

E2.3.1. Advantages of compound terms
Compound terms are more exact and specific than single terms used in combination to represent the same concept. They are able to prevent false drops and to ensure good precision.

For instance, a document on 'Fuels selection and water storage capacity in central heating systems' might be correctly indexed by the single terms FUELS, SELECTION, WATER, and STORAGE. It would be retrieved as an irrelevant document in a search for the concept 'Fuel storage' using in combination the single terms FUELS and STORAGE, but would be excluded by a search using the compound term FUEL STORAGE.

Another advantage of using compound terms is that the thesaurus displays information about the term (synonyms, broader, narrower and related terms, for example) which is lost if the compound term is factored, unless a special effort is made to show thesaural relationships against the non-preferred term (see 'Syntactical factoring' in E2.4.2(a)).

E2.3.2. Disadvantages of compound terms
A thesaurus with many highly pre-coordinated terms is more expensive to compile and maintain than one having a low pre-coordination level, because of its greater size and complexity. It also adds to indexing problems, as it is necessary to ensure that all the relevant specific, pre-coordinated terms have been assigned to the document. Use of compound terms can also lead to recall loss. This is more of a problem in manual systems, where a search for a part of a compound term rather than the whole term may not retrieve the document. For instance, a search for information on 'Boiler maintenance' using the terms BOILERS and MAINTENANCE would not retrieve documents indexed STEAM BOILERS and ENGINEERING MAINTENANCE, unless the indexer had 'posted up' to the generic term by indexing the document also under BOILERS and MAINTENANCE. In online searching, the document would be retrieved, as the constituent terms in compound terms may be retrieved independently if the controlled terms are searched using the free-text facility. That is, a search on BOILERS and MAINTENANCE would retrieve the term BOILERS in STEAM BOILERS and MAINTENANCE in ENGINEERING MAINTENANCE.

E2.3.3. Advantages of factored terms
Factored (also sometimes known as synthesized) terms give a better recall performance than compound terms in manual systems and allow for a smaller and less complex vocabulary. To be most effective the thesaurus should include a substantial entry vocabulary of lead-in terms from the compound form of the factored terms to the factored components.

E2.3.4. Disadvantages of factored terms
Factored terms give a poorer precision performance than compound terms because of their lack of specificity. Recall too may be lost if the entry vocabulary is not adequate. Without a good entry vocabulary, indexers and searchers may use a different combination of terms to represent a concept, resulting in recall failure.

Example:

Concept: Residual stress tests

Indexed: RESIDUAL STRESSES and MECHANICAL TESTING

Searched: RESIDUAL STRESSES and TESTS

This search would fail unless broadened to search TEST, truncated in natural language mode, with RESIDUAL STRESSES.

Another disadvantage is the loss of information in thesaural relationships (i.e. synonyms, broader, narrower and related terms) when the compound term is factored.

E2.4. Rules for the treatment of compound terms

The first Standard to contain detailed procedures for dealing consistently with compound terms was British Standard 5723, which was drafted by Derek Austin, designer of the PRECIS indexing system. The British Standard strongly influenced the second edition of the International Standard ISO 2788, which includes a section on compound terms very similar to that found in the British Standard.

E2.4.1. Retention of compound terms

The Standard suggests that the following classes of terms should be retained in their compound form.

(a) Proper names and terms containing proper names.

Examples:

SALVATION ARMY
LAKE DISTRICT
MARKOV PROCESSES
OEDIPUS COMPLEX

(b) Terms in which the difference has lost its original meaning.

Examples:

CABINET MAKING
MUNICIPAL ENGINEERING

Lancaster (46, Chapter 8) suggests that this rule should be extended to include the case in which the difference has no real meaning on its own.

Examples:

PULL TOYS
SPEECH DAYS

(c) Terms containing a difference which suggests a resemblance to an unrelated thing or event.

Examples:

TWILIGHT AREAS
BLACK ECONOMY

(d) Terms which cannot be re-expressed without the use of an extra noun (or nouns) that are present in the compound term only by implication.

Examples:

INTEREST HOLIDAYS
i.e. HOLIDAYS for PEOPLE with special INTERESTS

LANGUAGE LABORATORIES
i.e. Educational facilities providing AUDIOVISUAL AIDS for the
TEACHING of LANGUAGES.

(e) Terms in which the difference is not a valid species of the focus. 'The
noun in these cases is described as syncategorematic, since it cannot
stand alone as an indicator of the class of concepts to which the whole of
the term refers.'

Examples:

PINK ELEPHANTS
Not a species of elephant

RUBBER BONE
Not a species of bone

E2.4.2. Factoring of compound terms

E2.4.2.(a) Factoring techniques
There are two techniques for factoring compound terms – semantic
factoring and syntactical factoring.

○ Semantic factoring
This technique is applied to single as well as to compound terms. It is
defined in ISO 2788 as follows: 'A term which expresses a complex
notion is re-expressed in the form of simpler or definitional elements,
each of which can also occur in other combinations to represent a range
of different concepts'.

Example:

CARDIAC FAILURE
could be re-expressed by a combination of four terms
HEART + OUTPUT + BELOW + NORMAL

Semantic factoring leads to precision loss, and is not recommended by
ISO 2788, except for fringe subject areas.

○ Syntactical factoring
This technique is applied to compound terms which are 'amenable to
morphological analysis into separate components, each of which can be
accepted as an indexing term in its own right'.

Example:

COTTON SPINNING
factors into the two terms
COTTON + SPINNING

If the factored compound term is likely to be sought as a lead-in point,
the term as a whole should be entered in the thesaurus as a non-
preferred term, and a reference should be made to the components of
the term used in combination.

Example:

Cotton spinning
    USE COTTON + SPINNING

Reciprocal entries should be made from each term used in combination.

Example:

COTTON
  + SPINNING
  UF Cotton spinning

SPINNING
  + COTTON
  UF Cotton spinning

An alternative method of layout is found in *TEST* (Figure 6) and other thesauri modelled on it.

Example:

Cotton spinning
  USE COTTON AND SPINNING

COTTON
  UF †Cotton spinning

SPINNING
  UF †Cotton spinning

Definitions and thesaural relationships of factored compound terms (synthesized terms) are usually omitted, but it is possible to retain this information while indicating that the term is to be factored.

Example:

Day care of young people
  USE DAY CARE + YOUNG PEOPLE
  BT DAY CARE
  NT LATCHKEY PROVISION
  RT ALTERNATIVE EDUCATION
       INTERMEDIATE TREATMENT
       YOUNG PEOPLE

E2.4.2.(b) Factoring rules

The International Standard sets out recommendations for syntactical factoring, based upon general criteria. It is stressed that these recommendations are not regarded as mandatory instructions to be rigidly applied in all circumstances. Exceptions are permitted in particular situations. These are discussed in E2.4.2.(c) below.

○ Factoring Rule 1

The first rule recommends that 'a compound term should be factored if the focus refers to a property or part (including materials) and the difference represents the whole or a possessor of that property or part'.

Examples:

BICYCLE WHEELS
where BICYCLE is the containing whole and WHEELS is the part, factor:
BICYCLES + WHEELS

HOSPITAL FLOORS
where HOSPITAL is the containing whole and FLOORS is the part, factor:
HOSPITALS + FLOORS

INSTRUMENT RELIABILITY
where INSTRUMENT is the possessor of the property and
RELIABILITY is the property, factor:
INSTRUMENTS + RELIABILITY

The rule does allow, however, that 'the name of the thing may be
modified by its parts or property'.

Examples:

SPARE WHEELS
EMERGENCY HOSPITALS
PRECISION INSTRUMENTS

○ Factoring Rule 2
The second rule recommends that 'the name of a transitive action
should not be modified by the name of the patient on which the action is
performed'.

Examples:

GLASS CUTTING
where CUTTING is the transitive action and GLASS is the patient of
the action, factor:
GLASS + CUTTING

BEARING LUBRICATION
where LUBRICATION is the transitive action and BEARING is the
patient of the action, factor:
BEARINGS + LUBRICATION

PILOT TRAINING
where TRAINING is the transitive action and PILOT is the patient of
the action, factor:
PILOTS + TRAINING

Conversely, the rule allows that 'the name of a thing or material may be
modified by the name of the action carried out upon it'.

Examples:

CUT GLASS
LUBRICATED BEARINGS
TRAINED PILOTS

○ Factoring Rule 3
The third rule recommends that 'the name of an intransitive action
should not be modified by the name of the performer of the action'.

Examples:

BOILER EXPLOSIONS
where EXPLOSIONS is the intransitive action and BOILER is the
performer of the action, factor:
BOILERS + EXPLOSIONS

BEAM OSCILLATION
where OSCILLATION is the intransitive action and BEAM is the
performer of the action, factor:
BEAMS + OSCILLATION

DOCTOR EMIGRATION
where EMIGRATION is the intransitive action and DOCTOR is the performer of the action, factor:
DOCTORS + EMIGRATION

On the other hand, the rule allows that 'the name of the thing may be modified by the name of the intransitive action in which it is or was engaged'.

Example:

CORRODED BOILERS
OSCILLATING BEAMS
EMIGRATING DOCTORS

An additional rule, not included in the standard but suggested by Lancaster (46, Chapter 8) is that a compound term representing two different principles of division should always be factored.

Example:

UNDERWATER CINE CAMERAS
factors into
UNDERWATER CAMERAS + CINE CAMERAS

The differencing rules in the *PRECIS* manual (11) also reject as 'lead-terms' those compound terms which include 'a focus modified by more than one difference at the same level'.

Example (PRECIS manual, p.52):

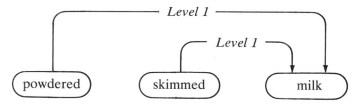

Compound lead-terms in the index:

POWDERED MILK
SKIMMED MILK
but not POWDERED SKIMMED MILK

However, if the differences are not at the same level, the full compound term can appear in the index.

Example (PRECIS manual, p.53):

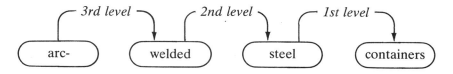

where Arc and Welded refer to Steel and not to Containers.

Compound lead-terms in the index:

ARC-WELDED STEEL CONTAINERS
WELDED STEEL CONTAINERS
STEEL CONTAINERS

E2.4.2.(c) Exceptions to the factoring rules

The International Standard ISO 2788 has three general rules which allow for the factoring rules to be overridden in certain circumstances, so relieving the compiler from constraints which might hinder the ability of the thesaurus to meet the requirements of a particular information system.

The first rule permits the factoring rules to be waived 'when the compound term has become so familiar in common use, or in the field covered by the thesaurus, that its expression as separate elements would hinder comprehension'.

Examples of terms in common use or familiar in certain special fields:

Breaking Factoring Rule 1

WOMENS RIGHTS
PIPE FITTINGS
GROUP STRUCTURE

Breaking Factoring Rule 2

PATIENT CARE
CHILD MINDING
WASTE DISPOSAL

Breaking Factoring Rule 3
DRUG INTERACTIONS
WORKER PARTICIPATION

The second rule permits overriding of the factoring rule when factoring would lead to a loss of meaning, or ambiguity.

Example:

GROUP + DISCUSSION
could be either
GROUP DISCUSSION or DISCUSSION GROUP
so the term is retained in the compound form although it breaks Factoring Rule 3.

The third rule states that factoring rules may be set aside 'when indexing in a special field requires special treatment'.

This rather general dispensation allows the factoring rules to be overlooked in a wide variety of situations. For example, compound terms may be retained in a system producing a printed index containing 'stand alone' terms rather than rotated terms in coordinated strings. In such an index the term HOUSING MANAGEMENT is more specific and helpful to the user than the separate, broader headings of HOUSING and MANAGEMENT, although the compound term breaks the second factoring rule. Compound terms may also have to be retained in an integrated thesaurus or switching language, where the 'master language' has to be as specific and pre-coordinated as the most detailed constituent language (see I2.1).

For instance, the *ECOT thesaurus* (70), intended as a switching language between databases on educational courses and occupations, has mapped onto it several thousand occupations from the *Classification of occupations and directory of occupational titles* (*CODOT*) (94). Many of these are compound terms which break the factoring rules, particularly Rule 2.

Example:

GLASS PACKAGING WORKERS
    SN   CODOT 841.25
    UF   Glass packers
    BT   Glass workers
          Packaging workers
    RT   Glass packaging

Where Glass packaging workers should be factored into GLASS and PACKAGING WORKERS, but the compound term exists at 841.25 in CODOT.

An alternative to retaining compound terms as full indexing terms in an integrated vocabulary or switching language is to indicate that the term is factored but to retain the thesaural relations (see 'Syntactical factoring' in E2.4.2), although this increases the complexity of thesaurus compilation and possibly the degree of confusion of the users.

Example:

Glass packaging workers

   USE GLASS
        + PACKAGING WORKERS
    UF   Glass packers
    BT   Glass workers
          Packaging workers

Section F

Structure: basic relationships and classification

An intrinsic feature of a thesaurus is its ability to distinguish and display the structural relationships between the terms it contains. In this section, the different types of relationship are identified, defined and illustrated, with reference to the Standards ISO 2788 and BS 5723. The associated topic of the display of relationships is treated in Section H.

There are two broad types of relationship in a thesaurus. The first is at the micro level and concerns the semantic links between individual terms. The three basic relationships, equivalence, hierarchical, and associative, are described in F1–3.

The second type of relationship is at the macro level, and concerns the relationships of sets of equivalent terms, and categories of hierarchical and associated terms, to one another and to the subject field as a whole. It is essential to study macro as well as micro level relationships if it is intended to produce a systematic display. It is also advisable, even if such a display is not intended, because an understanding of the structure at both levels will improve the quality of decisions made at the micro level concerning inter-term relationships. The two types of relationship tend to be interactive.

To determine inter-term groupings and the organization of these within the subject field, classificatory techniques are employed. These include classification in its broadest sense: 'arranging in classes according to a method' and classification with more specific meanings in information work, such as systematic classification and automatic classification. In systematic classification a sequence of classes is brought together and organized by a coding system, or notation. Faceted classification, described in F4, is a species of systematic classification, that uses facet analysis, a technique involving the allocation of concepts to their fundamental categories, applicable not only in subject field organization, but also in distinguishing different inter-term relationships.

Automatic classification, the use of statistical and linguistic techniques for the computer-aided generation of inter-term relationships, is discussed in F6.

F1. The equivalence relationship

As defined by the Standards BS 5723 and ISO 2788, this is 'the relationship between preferred and non-preferred terms where two or more terms are regarded, for indexing purposes, as referring to the same concept'. In other words, they form an equivalence set. The preferred term is the one chosen to represent the concept in indexing, while the non-preferred term (or terms) is the one not selected. The non-preferred terms form an 'entry vocabulary' directing the user from terms not selected to those which are. The following conventions are used to express the reciprocal relationship:

UF
(use for)
written as a prefix to the non-preferred term
USE
written as a prefix to the preferred term

Example:

PERMITTIVITY
  UF   Dielectric Constant

Dielectric Constant
  USE PERMITTIVITY

In the alphabetical display of a printed thesaurus (see H1), it is usual to distinguish typographically between the preferred and non-preferred terms.

The equivalence relation includes true synonyms and quasi-synonyms.

F1.1 Synonyms
The Standards define synonyms as 'terms whose meanings can be regarded as the same in a wide range of contexts, so that they are virtually interchangeable'. In general linguistics, synonyms are not common, but they do occur more frequently in scientific terminology. This is due to the proliferation of trade names and popular names and other variations depending on local usage and opinion or on etymological root. In all subject fields, not only scientific, there are more synonyms in controlled language than in natural language, because the meanings of terms are intentionally limited in controlled language.

There are several types of synonym. Those listed below are typical of true synonyms likely to occur in thesaurus-building.

○ Popular names and scientific names

Examples:

FLIP-FLOPS / BISTABLE MULTIVIBRATORS
SPIDERS / ARACHNIDA
MERCY KILLING / EUTHANASIA

○ Common nouns or scientific names, and trade names

Examples:

AMODIAQUINE / CAMOQUIN
POLYMETHYL METHACRYLATE / PERSPEX

○ Standard names and slang

Examples:

HIGH FIDELITY EQUIPMENT / HI-FI EQUIPMENT
SUPPLEMENTARY EARNINGS / PERKS

○ Variant spellings – including stem variants and irregular plurals

Examples:

GIPSIES / GYPSIES
MOSLEMS / MUSLIMS
MOUSE / MICE
FIBRE OPTICS / FIBER OPTICS
HAEMODYNAMICS / HEMODYNAMICS

The last two are examples of differences beween standard English and North American spelling.

○ Terms of different linguistic origin

Examples:

DOMICILIARY CARE / HOME CARE
ALIENS / FOREIGNERS
GEOMAGNETISM / TERRESTRIAL MAGNETISM
CAECITIS / TYPHLITIS

○ Terms originating from different cultures sharing a common language

Examples:

AERIALS / ANTENNA
POSTAL SERVICES / MAIL SERVICES
RAILWAYS / RAILROADS
PAVEMENTS / SIDEWALKS

○ Competing names for emerging concepts

Examples:

NON-ACCIDENTALLY INJURED CHILDREN / BATTERED
  CHILDREN
DISTANCE LEARNING / HOME LEARNING
AWARENESS GAMES / ICE BREAKERS

Once the pattern of usage clarifies, the preferred term may be changed. For example, LIFELONG EDUCATION is now usually preferred to CONTINUING EDUCATION, although both were popular at one time.

○ Current or favoured term versus outdated or deprecated term

Examples:

DISHWASHERS / WASHING-UP MACHINES
JOB CENTRES / EMPLOYMENT EXCHANGES
COMMUNITY HOMES / ORPHANAGES
HOVERCRAFT / AIR CUSHION VEHICLES / GROUND
  EFFECT VEHICLES

○ Abbreviations and full names

Examples:

ECG / ELECTROCARDIOGRAPHY
PPBS / PLANNING-PROGRAMMING-BUDGETING SYSTEMS
INDOR / INTERNUCLEAR DOUBLE RESONANCE

The full form of the term is usually preferred in a general index, but in a special field, where the abbreviated form is the most familiar, the abbreviation should be preferred, except where the same abbreviation stands for two different terms likely to occur in the same thesaurus.

Example:

BBC / BRITISH BROADCASTING CORPORATION
BBC / BROWN BOVERI COMPANY

Some acronyms are now so familiar that their original meaning has been lost. LASER, for example, could be shown without its full form 'Light amplification by stimulated emission of radiation' being given as an entry point.

○ The factored and unfactored forms of a compound term

Examples:

MILK HYGIENE / MILK and HYGIENE
PRISONERS FAMILIES / PRISONERS and FAMILIES

○ The direct and indirect forms of terms

Example:

ELECTRIC POWER PLANTS / POWER PLANTS, ELECTRIC

Entry under indirect form is required only where the focus of the compound term (POWER PLANTS in the example) is not an indexing term (see H1.3)

The selection of preferred terms from among possible synonyms should always be influenced by the needs of the users of the thesaurus. These will vary, depending on such factors as whether subjects are treated at a general or detailed level, or from the popular or specialist or scientific viewpoint. Whichever alternatives are adopted, they should be applied consistently throughout the thesaurus. Every effort should also be made to find all appropriate non-preferred synonyms for the preferred terms, in order to enrich the entry vocabulary and with it the usefulness of the thesaurus as a recall improvement device.

F1.2. Quasi-synonyms

Quasi-synonyms, also known as near-synonyms, are defined as terms whose meanings are generally regarded as different in ordinary usage, but they are treated as though they are synonyms for indexing purposes. Quasi-synonyms include terms having a significant overlap.

Examples:

URBAN AREAS / CITIES
CAR PARKS / PARKING SPACES
SPEECH IMPAIRED PEOPLE / STAMMERERS
GIFTED PEOPLE / GENIUSES

The acceptability of sets of terms as quasi-synonyms will be affected by the subject field covered by the thesaurus. For example, in a specialist thesaurus on Occupational Health, the terms INDUSTRIAL INJURY and OCCUPATIONAL INJURY might not be treated as synonymous, whereas in a more general thesaurus on Health Sciences they might be accepted as quasi-synonyms. The quasi-synonym device should be avoided as a means of reducing the size of the vocabulary by grouping together terms which ought to be treated as independent indexing terms, except in marginal subject areas.

Quasi-synonyms may also cover antonyms: terms that represent different viewpoints of the same property continuum.

Examples:

DRYNESS / WETNESS
HEIGHT / DEPTH
EQUALITY / INEQUALITY
LITERACY / ILLITERACY

If it is likely that a search on Literacy, for example, will always involve the examination of documents discussing both Literacy and its antonym, Illiteracy, the terms should be treated as quasi-synonyms. On the other hand, if a useful distinction can be made between two opposite terms, they should both be used as indexing terms and references made between them, otherwise precision may be lost.

F1.3. Upward posting

This is a technique which treats narrower terms as if they are equivalent to, rather than the species of, their broader terms. The effect is to reduce the size of the vocabulary, but at the same time to retain access via the specific terms to the broader terms used to represent them.

Examples:

THERMODYNAMIC PROPERTIES
  UF   Enthalpy
       Entropy
       Free energy
       Heat of adsorption
       etc.

Enthalpy
    USE THERMODYNAMIC PROPERTIES

Entropy
    USE THERMODYNAMIC PROPERTIES

etc.

SOCIAL CLASS
  UF   Elite
       Middle class
       Upper class
       Working class

Elite
    USE SOCIAL CLASS

Middle Class
    USE SOCIAL CLASS

etc.

AERIAL SPORTS
    UF   Gliding
           Hang gliding
           Parachuting
           Paragliding
           Sky diving
           etc.
Gliding
    USE AERIAL SPORTS
etc.

This device should be applied mainly in peripheral subject areas of the thesaurus, except in thesauri covering a wide range of subjects at a fairly low level of specificity.

Terms treated in this way as equivalent terms may be promoted later to the status of preferred indexing terms, if the frequency of occurrence of the terms in indexing and searching justifies it.

F2. The hierarchical relationship

This relationship shows 'levels of superordination and subordination. The superordinate term represents a class or whole, and the subordinate terms refer to its members or parts'. This relationship is used in locating broader and narrower concepts in a logically progressive sequence. It is a basic feature of the thesaurus, distinguishing it from unstructured term lists, and an important factor in the improvement of recall and also of precision performance.

The relationship is reciprocal and is set out in a thesaurus using the following conventions.

BT (i.e. broader term)
written as a prefix to the superordinate term

NT (i.e. narrower term)
written as a prefix to the subordinate term

Example:

PRIVATE ENTERPRISES
    BT   Enterprises

ENTERPRISES
    NT   Private enterprises

The hierarchical relationship includes the generic relationship, the hierarchical whole–part relationship, and the instance relationship. Terms are hierarchically related only if both are members of the same fundamental category, that is, they both represent entities, activities, agents or properties, etc. (See F4.)

In the example below, Curators and Museum techniques are agents and actions respectively and do not belong to the same fundamental category, i.e., entities, as the superordinate term Museums, and are therefore not NTs to it. They are, in fact, associated terms, discussed in the next section (F3.).

Example:

	Fundamental categories
MUSEUMS	Entity
Archaeological museums	Type of entity
Ethnographic museums	Type of entity
Curators	Agents
Museum techniques	Action
Scientific museums	Type of entity
Theatrical museums	Type of entity

It is important to remember that not all terms indented under a term in a faceted systematic display (see F4, H3.3) will be hierarchically related to the ones at the level above. They may be associatively related, and if so should be treated as such (see F3).

The display of hierarchies is considered in Section H and also in F4 and J7.2.1. Alphabetical displays usually show only one level of hierarchy under the superordinate term, but multiple level display is possible (see H1.2). In alphabetical displays it is usual to mix, in one sequence, subordinate terms characterized by different principles of division, whereas in systematic displays it is possible to achieve helpful subgroupings of homogeneous terms at the same hierarchical level. The subgroups are preceded by facet indicators (named 'node labels' in ISO 2788), which are described more fully in F4, H3.3, and J7.2.1 below.

Example:

Systematic display	**Alphabetical display**
PAINTS	PAINTS
	NT Cement paints
(By composition) ← Facet indicator	Oil paints
Oil paints	Primers
Water paints	Top coats
Cement paints	Undercoats
	Water paints
(By use) ← Facet indicator	
Primers	
Undercoats	
Top coats	

F2.1. The generic relationship

The Standards define this relationship as the one which 'identifies the link between a class or category and its members or species'. It has long been used in biological taxonomies, as in the first example below, but it is also applied between concepts in every subject field.

Examples:

VERTEBRATA
    NT Amphibia
          Aves
          Mammalia
          Pisces
          Reptilia

GASTROINTESTINAL AGENTS
NT   Antidiarrhoeals
      Anti-ulcer agents
      Bile acids
      Cathartics
      Digestants

INTERNAL COMBUSTION ENGINES
NT   Compression ignition engines
      Dual-fuel engines
      Gas engines
      Petrol engines
      Spark ignition engines

ONE-PARENT FAMILIES
NT   Fatherless families
      Motherless families

The generic relationship applies to types of actions, properties and agents, as well as to types of things (entities).

Examples:

HEAT TREATMENT
NT   Annealing
      Decarburization
      Hardening
      Tempering

THINKING
NT   Contemplation
      Divergent thinking
      Lateral thinking
      Reasoning

VALUE
NT   Cultural value
      Economic value
      Moral value
      Social value

TEACHERS
NT   Adult educators
      School teachers
      Special education teachers
      Student teachers

The relationship is correct if both the genus and the species are of the same fundamental category, as explained in F2 above. A further test is suggested in ISO 2788. This is the 'all-and-some' test for validity, as shown in the following diagram.

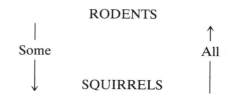

The diagram indicates that some members of the class of Rodents are Squirrels, while all Squirrels by definition, and regardless of context, are Rodents.

If, however, Squirrels is subordinated to a class such as Pests, the diagram shows that this is not invariably a true generic relationship, since some Pests are Squirrels, and only some Squirrels are Pests.

It is better to allocate Squirrels to the Rodent category, rather than to the inconstant Pests category, except perhaps in a thesaurus on Pest Control.

The Standard suggests that the generic relationship may be identified by the abbreviations NTG (narrow term generic) and BTG (broad term generic) or their equivalent in other languages.

Example:

CONVEYORS
  NTG   Belt conveyors

BELT CONVEYORS
  BTG   Conveyors

This special code would seem to be unnecessary to distinguish the generic from the hierarchical whole–part relationship, described below, as coding only the latter provides sufficient distinction.

F2.2. The hierarchical whole–part relationship
The whole–part relationship, except perhaps in a thesaurus in a narrow subject field, is regarded as an associative relationship. There are, however, a few circumstances where 'the name of the part implies the name of the possessing whole in any context'. The terms may then be regarded as a whole–part hierarchy. There are four instances admitted in the Standards.

a. Systems and organs of the body

Example:

EAR
  EXTERNAL EAR
  LABYRINTH
    SEMICIRCULAR CANALS
    VESTIBULAR APPARATUS
  MIDDLE EAR

b. Geographical location

Example:

ENGLAND
  WEST OF ENGLAND
    GLOUCESTERSHIRE
      COTSWOLD DISTRICT

c. Discipline or field of study

Example:

GEOLOGY
  ECONOMIC GEOLOGY
  ENGINEERING GEOLOGY
  PHYSICAL GEOLOGY
    PETROLOGY

d. Hierarchical social structure

Example:

METHODIST CHURCH ORGANIZATION
  METHODIST DISTRICT
    METHODIST CIRCUIT

The option is given in the Standard of using the following abbreviations, or their equivalents in other languages, to indicate the whole–part relationship:

BTP   Broader term (partitive)
NTP   Narrower term (partitive)

Example:

COTSWOLD DISTRICT
  BTP   Gloucestershire

GLOUCESTERSHIRE
  NTP   Cotswold District

F2.3. The instance relationship

This is the relationship between 'a general category of things and events, expressed by a common noun, and an individual instance of that category, the instance then forming a class of one which is represented by a proper name'. These proper names are identifiers, a class of term which is often excluded from the main part of the thesaurus, and is held in a separate file. However, when the identifier forms part of the thesaurus, the relationship between the identifier and its broader term is the instance relationship.

Example:

SEAS
  NT   Baltic Sea
       Caspian Sea
       Mediterranean Sea

since the Baltic Sea, Caspian Sea, etc., are not types, but instances of Seas.

F2.4. Polyhierarchical relationships

It is not unusual for terms to occur, equally correctly, under more than one category. The relationship between the term and its two or more superordinate terms is said to be polyhierarchical. This phenomenon may apply to both the generic and hierarchical whole–part terms.

Examples:

a. Generic

NURSES   HEALTH ADMINISTRATORS
  NT Nurse administrators   NT Nurse administrators

        NURSE ADMINISTRATORS
          BT Health administrators
              Nurses

b. Whole–part

EAST AFRICA   SOUTHERN AFRICA
  NT Zambia   NT Zambia

        ZAMBIA
          BT East Africa
              Southern Africa

c. Whole–part/generic

EAR   NERVES
  NT Acoustic nerve   NT Acoustic nerve

        ACOUSTIC NERVE
          BT Ear
              Nerves

        (Ear = whole–part; Nerves = generic relationship)

If some of the generic relationships possessed by the term are not 'true' generic relationships (see F2.1), they may still be considered poly-hierarchical and be treated as in the examples above.

F3. The associative relationship

The third basic relationship is less easy to define than the previous two. Put simply, the associative relationship is found between terms which are closely related conceptually but not hierarchically and are not members of an equivalence set. In other words, the terms are associated, but in a way other than described in the two previous paragraphs. The Standards state that associatively related terms (known as related terms) may be admitted if 'they are mentally associated to such an extent that the link between them should be made explicit in the thesaurus, on the grounds that it would reveal alternative terms which might be used for indexing and retrieval'. The relation is reciprocal, and is distinguished by the abbreviation 'RT' (related term).

Example:

TEACHING
  RT Teaching aids

TEACHING AIDS
  RT Teaching

There is always the risk that thesaurus compilers may overload the thesaurus with valueless relationships, which may impair precision performance without much improving recall. To overcome this tendency, the Standard recommends that 'one of the terms should be strongly implied, according to the frames of reference shared by the users of the index, whenever the other is employed as an indexing term'. The Standard goes on to suggest that where terms are closely related 'it will frequently be found that one of the terms is a necessary component in any definition or explanation of the other'. For example, the term Teaching is needed to define the term Teaching aids, but not vice versa. The Standard does not go so far as to recommend that relationships are invalid if this definition test is failed although this principle is applied in PRECIS. Subjective relationships are more likely to occur in specialized fields for a particular type of clientele. For example, a link between the terms Divorce and Legal aid appears in the 'Community information classification' (80), because research on terms appearing in enquiries put to community information agencies showed a strong co-occurrence between these terms. In a thesaurus with a different clientele, such a relationship would not be justified.

There are two types of associative relationship, those that belong to the same, and those that belong to different, categories.

F3.1. Terms belonging to the same category

It is not necessary, as a general rule, to relate terms belonging to the same class or genus, i.e., sibling terms. The relationship may be seen by scanning the systematic display, if one exists, or by checking the relevant broader term in the alphabetical display, which will list all the sibling terms at the same level as the sought term.

Example:

Term sought: Radial bearings

RADIAL BEARINGS JCK
   BT   Bearings
   RT   Plain bearings ⎫
         Rolling bearings ⎬ not necessary

Find related siblings by checking JCK or BT = BEARINGS.

Systematic display	*Alphabetical display*
JC Bearings	BEARINGS JC
JCC Plain bearings	NT Plain bearings
JCC.D Sliding bearings	Radial bearings ←
JCF Rolling bearings	Roller bearings
JCF.B Ball bearings	
→ JCK Radial bearings	

The Standards suggest that exceptions should be made to this rule when the sibling terms have overlapping meanings and are sometimes used loosely and almost interchangeably, even though each of the terms is amenable to an exact definition, and consequently they do not form an equivalent set. The Standard gives as an example, Ships and Boats, which are both species of the genus Vessels. Pairs of siblings may also be related if they have some particularly strong link between them, which does not occur between other members of the same species.

F3.2. Terms belonging to different categories

Much effort has gone into work on classifying associative relationships into different categories. The Standards list some of the most frequently mentioned. These are given below with some others encountered in practice.

a. The whole–part associative relationship

Apart from the four instances of hierarchical whole–part relationships listed above (F2.2), the whole–part relationship is associative, since this is a link between terms in different fundamental categories. This relationship is fairly easy to recognize, particularly when concrete objects are involved.

Examples:

NUCLEAR REACTORS
  RT   Pressure vessels

OPERATING THEATRES
  RT   Surgical equipment

BUILDINGS
  RT   Doors

ISO 2788 allows that in a highly specialized thesaurus the whole–part relationship may be treated as hierarchical if the 'name of the whole is implied by the name of the part'. For instance, a thesaurus in the field of Fan Engineering, in which the term Blades might be shown as NT and not RT to the term Fans, because in this limited field other applications of the term Blades would not occur. However, there is less likelihood of inconsistency in the determination of whole–part relationships, if the hierarchical whole–part relationship is reserved for the four categories given above in F2.2.

b. A discipline or field of study and the objects or phenomena studied

Examples:

SEISMOLOGY
  RT   Earthquakes

ONCOLOGY
  RT   Neoplasms

MECHANICAL ENGINEERING
  RT   Prime movers

ETHNOGRAPHY
  RT   Primitive societies

c. An operation or process and the agent or instrument

Examples:

VELOCITY MEASUREMENT
  RT   Speedometers

TURNING
  RT   Lathes

MOTOR RACING
  RT   Racing cars

HAIRDRESSING
  RT   Hair driers

d. An occupation and the person in that occupation

Examples:

ACCOUNTANCY
RT   Accountants

SOCIAL WORK
RT   Social workers

BRICKLAYING
RT   Bricklayers

SPORT
RT   Professional sportsmen

e. An action and the product of the action

Examples:

SCIENTIFIC RESEARCH
RT   Scientific inventions

ROADMAKING
RT   Roads

VIOLENCE
RT   Violence victims

PUBLISHING
RT   Music scores

f. An action and its patient

Examples:

DRIVING
RT   Road vehicles

DATA ANALYSIS
RT   Data

TEACHING
RT   Students

ART THERAPY
RT   Psychiatric patients

g. Concepts related to their properties

Examples:

SURFACES
RT   Surface properties

STEEL ALLOYS
RT   Corrosion resistance

WOMEN
RT   Femininity

h. Concepts related to their origins

Examples:

WATER
RT   Water wells

INFORMATION
RT   Information sources

i. Concepts linked by causal dependence

Examples:

EROSION
  RT Wear

INJURY
  RT Accidents

j. A thing or action and its counter-agent

Examples:

PESTS
  RT Pesticides

CORROSION
  RT Corrosion inhibitors

CRIME
  RT Crime prevention devices

k. A raw material and its product

Examples:

AGGREGATES
  RT Concretes

HIDES
  RT Leather

l. An action and a property associated with it

Examples:

PRECISION MEASUREMENT
  RT Accuracy

COMMUNICATION
  RT Communication skills

m. A concept and its opposite (antonym not treated as quasi-synonym)

Examples:

SINGLE PEOPLE
  RT Married people

TOLERANCE
  RT Prejudice

Although it is useful to be aware of the above varieties of related terms, and others not mentioned here, the compiler need establish only that the relationship falls into the broad category of related term. This may be done by applying the validation tests set out in F2. (If these show that the terms are not hierarchically related they must be related terms.) On the whole, it is easier to judge the correct relationship between terms in the pure sciences and technology than in the social sciences and humanities. Compilers should look out for a common error in manually produced thesauri, when both BT and RT relationships occur between the same pair of terms. The mistake arises when the compiler makes a different decision about the relationship when handling the second term than was made, some time earlier, when handling the first term. This is usually due to the relevant reciprocal entry either not having been generated or becoming mislaid.

F3.3. Related terms in the systematic display

When a thesaurus includes a systematic display (see H3.3), related terms are shown in the schedules in two ways, either indented under a superordinate related term, as if they were species or members of a hierarchy, or listed as a cross-reference under the reciprocally related terms.

F3.3.1. Indenting under superordinate related term

Example:

LF		Fire
		(Risks)
LFD	*(RT)*	Fire risks
LFD.F	*(RT)*	Flammable atmospheres
		(Safety measures)
LFH	*(RT)*	Fire safety
		(Firefighting measures)
LFP	*(RT)*	Firefighting
		(Equipment)
LFP.C	*(RT)*	Firefighting equipment
LFP.CC	*(RT)*	Fire hoses

In the above example, all the terms indented one level below the term Fire are associatively and not hierarchically related to it. They are coded RT accordingly, so that the correct relationship will be shown between the terms in the alphabetical display. That is:

FIRE
   RT   Fire fighting
         Fire risks
         Fire safety

The RT may be omitted from the printed systematic display.

Displays with associated terms and hierarchically related terms mixed in the same schedule are those organized to give an overview of the contents of a subject field or discipline. This will inevitably include some terms from different fundamental categories (see F4) which are not generically related.

It is important not to confuse schedule subordination with hierarchical subordination in the systematic display.

F3.3.2. Cross-references between related terms in different classes and hierarchies

In the example below, the term Fire insurance appears in a different subject field, that is, under Insurance. Reciprocal references are made between the related terms, each cross-reference preceded by the abbreviation RT (or sometimes *RT). (Systematic displays are covered in more detail in sections F4, H3.3, J7.2.1, and J7.3.)

Example:

LF		**Fire**
		RT Fire insurance TVH
		(Risks)
LFD	*(RT)*	Fire risks
...		
TV		**Insurance**
		...
TVH		Fire insurance
		RT Fire LF

F4. Faceted classification

A faceted classification is a type of systematic classification using analytico-synthetic techniques. It is synthetic because it makes provision for concept-building, to represent topics which are not specifically enumerated, and analytical because it is structured in such a way that the class numbers represent simple concepts, organized into clearly defined categories during a rigorous process known as facet analysis. A faceted classification is similar in structure to a thesaurus, and is unlike enumerative classification systems, which deal in complex terms and phrases and have only a limited facility for combining with one another. The affinity between faceted classification schemes and thesauri means that faceted classification is useful in thesaurus construction in two ways. First, it provides a tool for the analysis of subject fields and for determining the relationships between the concepts therein. (See also J7.) Second, the resulting faceted classification may be used as the systematic display in the published thesaurus (see H3.3).

There are a number of published thesauri which use facet analysis as a construction technique, and contain faceted displays. The layout of some of these is discussed in H3.3. Faceted classification schemes in special subject areas are a useful source of terminology and structure. In addition, there is the second edition of the Bliss Classification (BC2), which is a fount of detailed terminology, analysed and organized within subject fields by facet techniques. The first edition of the Bliss Classification appeared between 1940 and 1953, the result of a lifetime of study by its compiler, H.E. Bliss. It was notable for its carefully planned main classes, alternative places, short notation and some synthetic qualities. The second edition (97), edited by Jack Mills and Vanda Broughton, and supported by the Bliss Classification Association, is in course of development. The original shell of the system remains, with minimum change, and within each class the schedules are designed on facet principles. In the introductory volume and elsewhere, Jack Mills has described the underlying philosophy. The plan is to produce BC2 in separate parts for individual main classes, each with its own introduction, schedule and index. By 1986, volumes for seven main classes had been published, several more were nearing completion and the rest in draft form or in process of drafting. The unpublished drafts are available to those wishing to adapt or extract data from the schedules. The Bliss Classification Association encourages this use of the system as a source of terms and structure for special classification schemes or thesauri, so long as due acknowledgement is made in any publication which results. For thesaurus purposes, the detail in the schedules has to be edited, to introduce more precision into word form control and into recognizing and labelling the hierarchical, polyhierarchical, associative relationships present. (See article by Aitchison (1) on the use of Bliss as a thesaurus resource in the development of the *DHSS-DATA thesaurus* and others.)

The distinctive feature of a faceted classification is the division of terms into subclasses, or facets, using only one characteristic (or principle) of division at a time, to produce homogeneous, mutually exclusive groups. There is an underlying pattern of fundamental categories in all subject fields, which are represented in the facets analysed. Fundamental categories were first named by S. R. Ranganathan, the originator of analytico-synthetic classification and in particular *The Colon Classification* (58). He listed five fundamental categories, 'Personality', 'Matter', 'Energy', 'Space', and 'Time' (PMEST). 'Space', 'Time' and 'Matter' are self-explanatory. 'Energy' is a category representing activities, processes and problems. 'Personality' is difficult to define, but represents the key facet, which may include things, kinds of things, or actions and kinds of actions, depending on the bias of the subject field. Over several years of research and discussion, the theory of fundamental categories has developed and they are now usually considered to include:

Entities (things, objects)
  (Abstract/concrete)
  Abstract entities
  Concrete entities
    Naturally occurring substances
    Artefacts (man-made)

  (By function)
  Agents (Performers of action – inanimate and animate)
  Patients (Recipients of action – inanimate and animate)
  End-products

  (By characteristics)
  Properties
  Materials, constituent substances
  Parts
  Whole entities
  Complex entities

Actions
  Processes (internal processes, intransitive actions)
  Operations (external, transitive actions)
  Complex actions

Space

Time

In addition, Kinds or Types; Systems and Assemblies; Applications and Purposes of the above categories.

A special adaptation of these fundamental categories is found in the *PRECIS* subject indexing system (11), where they are used in a closely defined and strictly controlled way as role operators, to determine the order of terms in a pre-coordinate index. The primary operators include (0) Location, (1) Key system, (2) Action/Effect, and (3) Performer of transitive action (agent), representing fundamental categories Space, Things (when action not present, or toward which an action is directed), Action, and Agent respectively; while among the secondary operators are the categories Part, Property, Types, and Systems in the operators (p) Part or Property, (q) Member of a quasi-generic group, and (r) Assembly.

When analysing a subject field, concepts are first divided into broad facets, representing the fundamental categories. For example, in the field of Clothing Technology, the broad facets might include 'end-products', 'parts', 'properties', 'operations', and 'agents' (human and machine). The broad facets are further analysed and appropriate terms allocated to each. These terms are then sorted into subfacets (also known as arrays). The Clothing Technology schedule in Figure 3 shows that the *end-product* facet, Clothing, may be divided by *type*; according to *process used*: Knitwear; by *property*: Lightweight clothing; by *purpose*: Outerwear, Nightwear; by *user*: Baby clothing, Womens clothing. The *parts* facet might contain Collars, Sleeves, Linings, etc., and the *materials* facet Textile fabrics, Leather, and other substances. The *operations* facet might cover manufacturing processes, such as Patternmaking, Cutting, Sewing, and special skills such as Tailoring. The *agents* facet might be represented by Clothing technology equipment and human agents, Clothing personnel, those involved in the clothing industry. The subfacets may be divided by a second round of concepts representing the fundamental categories, and these may be divided by a third round, and so on. For example Womens clothing may be classified by 'type' according to purpose, Maternity wear, while a further round might distinguish a 'property', Maternity wear sizes. This operation of 'judging the correct relationship that each term has to the general class and assigning it accordingly' is what facet analysis entails. As each facet and subfacet is identified, it is preceded by a facet indicator (also known as a node label), which labels the facet by its characteristic of division.

The filing order, or the order of the arrangement of facets within a subject field, is preferably in the order of increasing specificity, complexity and concreteness. Put in other ways the schedules show an evolutionary order, or place 'means before ends'. In a faceted thesaurus for post-coordinate use, the order of the facets is not crucial, but in pre-coordinated system applications, where the filing order affects the citation order, it has significance. The citation order is the order in which the concepts in the faceted schedule are cited in a compound class mark or string of terms in a pre-coordinated index. In the Clothing technology schedule in Figure 3 the citation order would be the reverse of the filing order.

Filing order	*Citation order*
Agents	End-products
Operations	Parts
Materials	Materials
Parts	Operations
End-products	Agents

Figure 3. Faceted classification

M	CLOTHING TECHNOLOGY
	(Personnel)
MC	Clothing technology personnel
MCE	Clothing technology managers
MCP	Clothing workers
MCP.D	Sewing machinists
	(Equipment)
ME	Clothing technology equipment
MEH	Sewing machines
	(Operations)
MG	Clothing manufacturing processes
MGH	Patternmaking
MGJ	Cutting
MGL	Sewing
MGT	Tailoring
MGV	Dressmaking
	(Materials)
MI	Clothing materials
MIK	Textile fabrics
MIR	Leather
MIV	Fur
	(Parts)
MKL	Collars
MKP	Sleeves
MKQ	Cuffs
MKV	Linings
	(End-products)
MM	Clothing
	(By process used)
MNP	Knitwear
	(By property)
MOR	Lightweight clothing
	(By material)
MPI.T	Woollen clothing
MPI.V	Fur clothing
	(By purpose)
MQQ	Outerwear
MQQ.C	Coats
MQQ.H	Dresses
MQQ.N	Suits
MQR	Hosiery
MQS	Headwear
MQT	Footwear
MQU	Underwear
MSN	Nightwear
MST	Sportswear
MTU	Uniforms
	(By user)
MVC	Baby clothing
MVE	Childrens clothing
MVM	Womens clothing
MVM.P	Maternity wear
MVR	Mens clothing

A compound subject, for example, 'Clothing workers engaged in patternmaking for womens clothing', would be expressed by citing class marks (or their equivalent terms) in the following order:

End-product	*Operation*	*Agent*
MVM	MGH	MCP
Womens clothing	Patternmaking	Clothing workers

In the compound class mark, or string of terms, only the preferred or first-cited class mark or term is accessible in the lead position. Rotating the terms or elements of the class mark ensures that each concept is given priority in turn.

A thesaurus lacking an in-built citation order may still be used pre-coordinately, by imposing an order extraneous to the schedules, such as the *PRECIS* role operators (11).

Example:

PRECIS role operators
(1)　Key system (thing towards which an action is directed)
(2)　Action
(3)　Performer of transitive action (agent)

Application of operators
(1)　Womens clothing
(2)　Patternmaking
(3)　Clothing workers

Entries ('shunted' according to *PRECIS* rules)
　Womens clothing.
　　Patternmaking.　Clothing workers.
　Patternmaking.　Womens clothing.
　　Clothing workers.
　Clothing workers.　Patternmaking.　Womens clothing.

Although the order of terms in a faceted classification used in a thesaurus post-coordinately is less significant than for one used pre-coordinately, it is still helpful for the compiler and the user if a consistent pattern may be discerned, at least in similar subject fields. The 'general to specific' order is the most likely to be generally acceptable. A possible standard arrangement for the facets of a subject field or discipline might be as follows:

Common subdivisions
　Document form
　Time. Historical aspects
　Space. Place subdivisions
　Research, education, communication, and information in the subject; administrative and legal aspects
Influence of/relations with other fields
Principles and theory
Agents
　Persons and organizations
　Facilities and equipment
Actions
　Processes
　Operations

Properties
Materials
Parts
Whole entities
Systems of entities

This order need not be strictly adhered to, and may be modified to suit special situations. For instance, Administration in Social Welfare may need to be treated as a major operations facet and be moved from its place under common subdivisions. It is nevertheless useful to the compiler to have as a reference point an agreed underlying order. The influence of BC2 may be seen in the above arrangement. A similar list of categories, but with a somewhat different filing order, is found in the 'Systematifier', intended as a standard for the organization of subject fields, developed by Dahlberg (23), after the analysis of the content of several hundreds of fields. The order of facets in the faceted type of thesaurus, Classaurus, developed by Bhattacharyya (13) is also not unlike the one given above, except that the Whole entities precede the Properties and Actions.

The order of concepts within subfacets may follow the same pattern as within the broad facets, where this is helpful. For instance, in Figure 3 the subfacets under Clothing are arranged according to type, in the same standard order as the broad facets, 'By process used' preceding 'By property' and 'By material'.

A faceted classification possesses synthetic qualities because its class marks (and corresponding terms) are free to combine with one another, whether the class marks or terms are combined at the searching stage, post-coordinately, or pre-coordinately, in class marks for shelving purposes, or in an index string of terms. A faceted classification, in addition, may be designed so that new concepts, whether single terms or compound terms, may be built up by combining existing class marks rather than enumerating the concept. This gives the classification a measure of self-updating. For example, in Figure 3 the concept of 'Tailor' could be expressed by combining the class mark MCP Clothing workers, with the class mark Tailoring MGT, to give the compound class mark MGT:MCP (or MGT.CP if retroactive notation, described in F5, is used). If the new concept is a compound term, it should not be retained in this form if it runs counter to the compound term factoring rules. The two class marks and their equivalent terms should be left as separate entities. For example, the compound term Fur clothing may be built up by combining Fur MIV with Clothing (by material) MP to give the compound class mark MP:MIV (or MPI.V with retroactive notation), but the compound term Sleeve cutting MKL:MGL (or MKL GL) should not be made by combining Sleeves MKP and Cutting MGJ, as this is not acceptable according to the rules. (See E2.4.2 (b), Factoring Rule 2.)

Faceted schedules which show a consistent 'general before special' order, as in the example in Figure 3, allow all later concepts to be qualified by those which occur earlier in the schedules. If this is done consistently, terms will be placed specifically with the concepts they qualify. For example, Sewing machines is 'brought down' to appear under Sewing at MGL.E and not earlier in the schedule under Clothing equipment at MEH, and Sewing machinists is 'brought down' to appear under Sewing machines at MGL.ECP rather than earlier in the schedule at Clothing workers MCP.D. When used as the systematic display of a thesaurus, a reference must be made from the earlier location in the schedule for the term to its specific place later, or the term may be entered in both places (see also H3.3.3).

Example:

MCP	Clothing workers
	*NT Sewing machinists MGL.EC
ME	Clothing technology equipment
	*NT Sewing machines MGL.E
MG	Clothing manufacturing processes
	...
MGL	Sewing
	(Equipment)
MGL.E	Sewing machines
	*BT Clothing technology equipment ME
	(Operators)
MGL.ECP	Sewing machinists
	*BT Clothing workers MCP

(Note: The class marks MGL.E, MGL.ECP are built up retroactively by 'bringing down' the E and CP from ME and MCP. See F5.)

In a faceted thesaurus display it would be equally valid to leave Sewing machines under Clothing technology equipment, and Sewing machinists under Clothing workers, and to show the associative relationship between Sewing machines and Sewing, and Sewing machinists and Sewing machines by RT references.

Example:

MCP	Clothing workers
MCP.D	Sewing machinists
	*RT Sewing machines MEH
ME	Clothing technology equipment
MEH	Sewing machines
	*RT Sewing MGL
	Sewing machinists MCP. D
	...
MG	Clothing manufacturing processes
MGL	Sewing
	*RT Sewing machines MEH

If this latter pattern is preferred, then the earlier concepts are being qualified by the later and not vice versa, Clothing workers by equipment used, Sewing machines and Clothing technology equipment by process used, Sewing.

In this section, facet analysis has been considered only at the level of subdivision of a main class or special field. There is also the question of how to organize a systematic classification for the total subject area of the thesaurus, which may cover more than one main field and also subsidiary fields. Division of the whole subject of the thesaurus could be by subject field and discipline or by fundamental facets. These alternatives are discussed in J7.1. For further reading on faceted classification see items 2, 10, 16, 20, 30, 31, 58, 69, 97 in the bibliography.

F5. Notation

The main function of the notation, a set of symbols added to the classification system, is to represent the concepts and give each one a filing value in a self-evident order. Symbols commonly used in notation are Arabic numerals and the Roman alphabet (small letters and capitals), which have a widely recognized filing order. Other symbols are used, such as hyphens, colons, and oblique signs, with an imposed arbitrary order, as they lack an obvious value.

A possible secondary function of notation is to express the hierarchy of the classes, showing subordinate classes (subclasses) and coordinate classes (equal classes). A notation which attempts to show hierarchy is known as an expressive or hierarchical notation and one which does not is a non-expressive or ordinal notation. An expressive notation may be used in online searches to retrieve all documents classified by notation more specific than the cut-off point of a truncated class mark.

In practice, although it is possible to maintain a notation which shows every step of the hierarchy, the principle will break down when the subclasses of any genus out-number the characters available in the notation. This may be as few as ten in a conventional decimal notation, although twenty-six in an alphabetical notation of capital letters only. Expressive notations are also 'inhospitable'. This means they do not easily allow the interpolation of new concepts, because of the rigidity of the structure. In the example below, it is not possible to insert a new concept at the same hierarchical level between Fire at 831 and Explosions at 832. Lack of hospitality is more pronounced in ten-place decimal notations than in alphabetical notations. However, where a lengthy class mark may be tolerated, numerical notations exist which are expressive, hospitable and can be used for online 'exploded' class mark searches, as found in *MeSH* (95) and other thesauri. These use 3-digit numerical systems, which allow up to 100 places at each hierarchical level. If this type of notation were used to express Carbon dioxide fire extinguishers in the example below, the class mark could be as long as:

$$830.500.650.405.260.40$$

to cover the five hierarchical steps separating it from its generic term Hazards.

A common practice is to adopt an ordinal or semi-ordinal notation which ensures a generally shorter class mark, because the notation can more easily be evenly distributed throughout the scheme, and allows new concepts to be inserted in the correct place, when required. For instance, HNY might be used in the example below to represent the hazard Dangerous environments inserted between Fire and Explosions.

Example:

Expressive notation

83	Hazards
831	Fire
831.5	Firefighting
831.53	Firefighting equipment
831.532	Fire extinguishers
831.532.5	Carbon dioxide fire extinguishers
832	Explosions

Ordinal notation

HK	Hazards
HL	Fire
HM	Firefighting
HN	Firefighting equipment
HNB	Fire extinguishers
HNE	Carbon dioxide fire extinguishers
HNY	Dangerous environments
HO	Explosions

When an ordinal notation is used, the indenting of the text of the classification is the sole indicator of hierarchical levels, unless the notation is itself indented, as is done in the *Thesaurus of consumer affairs* (77).

Example:

D100   Production
.D105   Production methods
..D107   Automation

Another advantage of the ordinal notation is that it is possible to give a brief class mark to important concepts which are in a subordinate position in a hierarchy. The following examples are taken from the *British catalogue of music classification* (84) and from BC2 (97).

Examples:

PW   Keyboard instruments
Q   Piano
R   Organ

TSY Financial administration
TT   Accountancy

Most ordinal notations do show an element of hierarchy and are in fact semi-ordinal. This usually appears in the lower levels of division. The *ROOT thesaurus* (81), for example, has a notation which is ordinal when representing the broader subclasses and expressive for narrower terms. The structure of the broader classes is shown by indicating the range of marks used to cover the hierarchical step.

Example:

KB/KO	Electrical engineering
KE/KJ	Electrical equipment
KF	Electric machines
KFT	Electric motors
KFT.C	Alternating current motors
KFT.CD	Synchronous motors

This type of notation gives a medium-length class mark, while showing to some extent the structure of the scheme. This expressiveness gives way to the ordinal approach when the number of subclasses exceeds the characters available or the reflection of the hierarchical steps would prevent the insertion of a new concept at the correct place.

Hospitality, which allows the system to grow and absorb new concepts, is another essential quality of a notation. The insertion of new concepts within arrays is easily achieved if an ordinal notation is used, as has been seen. Another way of achieving hospitality is by using synthesis in notation, which allows the combining of symbols representing concepts in one facet or array with those of others. Such synthesized class marks should only be used in a thesaurus when the equivalent terms would not be factored, according to the rules (see E2.4.2). Some thesauri have common terms in auxiliary schedules which may be used throughout the scheme to build new concepts.

Example:

Synthesis using Common Terms		**Enumeration**	
AT	Information	P	Architecture
ATM	Information services	PB	Architectural information
		PBM	Architectural information services
P	Architecture		
PAT	Architectural information		
PAT.M	Architectural information services		

The use of the synthetic device makes the scheme, in part, self-updating, and saves notation which can then be used for subclasses which have to be enumerated. On the other hand, a synthesized class number is usually longer than an enumerated one as is the case in the example above.

A device known as retroactive notation is used in some faceted classifications to shorten the synthesized class marks. Any notation following at some later point in an array or subdivision of a field may be assigned the subnotation of some earlier subdivision, so as to indicate its own subdivision. In this way, compound concepts are built up 'backwards' – hence 'retroactive'. The schedules have to be designed so that the more general concepts appear in the earlier part of the schedules to qualify the more specific concepts later in the sequence. The class marks are short because the facet indicator from the earlier notation is dropped when this is added to the later, as is illustrated in Figure 3 above, and also in the first example on page 56 of F4 above. The following example is from BC2(95), which has a retroactive notation throughout.

Example:

QL   Children
             ...
QLV   Old people
             ...
QM   Handicapped people
             ...
QMP   Mentally handicapped people
QMP L   Mentally handicapped children
QMP LV   Mentally handicapped old people

Retroactive notation should not be used to synthesize compound terms which would be better factored for thesaurus purposes.

Example:

QD   Social work
             ...
QL   Children
             ...
QLD   Social work with children

QLD produces an unacceptable compound term, breaking the second factoring rule (see E2.4.2) that a transitive action is not qualified by the patient of the action.

The choice and allocation of the notation should be, it is again emphasized, a secondary process to the major one of arranging the concepts of the classification, and is usually deferred until after the classification is completed. On the other hand, a poorly designed notation can reduce the value of the best constructed scheme.

F6. Automatic generation of indexing languages

Automatic thesaurus construction is one component of the wider field of automatic information retrieval which also encompasses automatic indexing, automatic abstracting and automatic document classification. In all these operations, statistical techniques or computational linguistics replace human intellectual processes. Research in the whole field has been reviewed by Stevens (67) and Sparck Jones (65, 66).

Automatic extraction indexing, that is the automatic selection of words and phrases to represent the content of the document, has been shown to be a viable indexing aid for an operational situation. The application of this technique in the selection of candidate terms for conventionally compiled thesauri is mentioned later (J5.2.2).

Another indexing aid which shows real promise for operational information systems is automatic assignment indexing. Using this technique, classification codes and indexing terms from a limited humanly compiled vocabulary or thesaurus are assigned to a document if they match, above some statistical threshold, the automatically extracted words and phrases (5).

The use of automatic techniques in the construction of thesauri has not yet found regular application in an operational situation. In the automatic generation of thesauri, relationships between indexing terms are identified statistically rather than semantically. The computer is programmed to form clusters of related terms on the basis of the co-occurrence of words derived from a corpus of text. Automatically constructed thesauri are of two types, those which are created as an 'internal thesaurus' from the processed text before searching, as illustrated in the work of Salton (60), and those which do not require calculation of association prior to the search, thus economizing on computer processing time. In this latter approach, developed by Doszkocs (26) and Doszkocs and Rapp (27), the source of the thesaurus is found in the words associated with the documents retrieved on processing the query against the database. Terms are considered for the thesaurus only if they occur in the retrieved set more frequently than in the database as a whole. The purpose of these thesauri is to improve retrieval performance by substituting the appropriate cluster of terms for one of its members. The heterogeneous nature of the clusters makes it more likely that recall rather than precision will be enhanced.

A more detailed account of the approach to automatic thesaurus construction is found in Lancaster (46, Chapter 21).

Section G

Auxiliary retrieval devices

Auxiliary retrieval devices are those syntactical tools which exist independently of the vocabulary. They should be distinguished from devices such as specificity and compound terms which are an integral part of the vocabulary.

G1. Post-coordination and pre-coordination

Coordination of terms in indexing and searching is a powerful device in retrieval. Precision is improved by increasing the number of terms combined in a search, and recall is improved by reducing the number. By combining A and B, greater specificity and precision is achieved than if A or B is treated alone.

In a post-coordinate system (usually a computer database, but also including punched card and optical coincidence systems), the indexing terms allocated to the document are not combined with one another but remain independent. At the searching stage, a request for any combination of these terms can be met. As Lancaster puts it (46, Chapter 2), a 'multidimensionality of relationship' amongst the terms is retained. For example, the phrase 'Testing the sound level of audiology rooms in hospitals' consists of four concepts: 'Audiology rooms', 'Sound level', 'Testing' and 'Hospitals'. If all four terms are asked for in combination, the highest level of coordination, and therefore of precision, is achieved. Documents which do not include testing, for example, or are concerned with audiology rooms not in the hospital environment are excluded. There is always the danger of recall loss with high pre-coordination. Some excluded documents might have been relevant, but the indexer in one document might have omitted the term 'Hospital', and in another might have used the term 'Examination' rather than 'Testing'. By reducing the coordination level to the three terms 'Audiology rooms' 'Sound level' and 'Testing', the first document is retrieved, and by reducing the level to two ('Audiology rooms' and 'Sound level'), the second omitted relevant document is also recalled.

In pre-coordinate systems, such as printed indexes, or library subject catalogue entries, terms are combined by the indexer, and are not free to respond to every combination of terms required by the searcher. The terms are combined in a linear 'string', so that the searcher has not only to match the terms used, but also the order within the 'string'. For example, the document on 'Testing the sound levels of audiology rooms in hospitals' might be indexed in the term order 'Audiology rooms': 'Sound levels': 'Testing': 'Hospitals'. A broad search on 'Audiology rooms' would retrieve the document, and all other documents with the term in the lead position, but searches on the other terms in the string would not retrieve the document, unless the terms in the string were rotated to bring each term into the lead position. If the search is to be made more precise by increasing the coordination level, the chances of matching the order of the terms in the indexing decreases with the number of terms in combination in the search. A search with terms in the order 'Audiology rooms': 'Hospitals': 'Sound levels': 'Testing' would not retrieve the document mentioned above, for example, which is indexed by the same terms but combined differently. This limitation is partially overcome by restricted rotation of terms in the subordinate positions in the 'string'. Full permutation of the terms would increase unacceptably the size of the printed index.

G2. Post-coordinate searching devices

There are a number of devices which are an essential part of post-coordinate search strategies. All of these may be used with controlled as well as natural language systems. Although these devices are entirely independent of the vocabulary, their application alongside the terminology in searching justifies a mention of them here in this manual. Weighting as a searching device is discussed under G6 below.

G2.1. Logical operators

Post-coordinate systems provide a means of combining search topics into logical groups with the Boolean operators: *OR, AND,* and *NOT.*

The *OR* operator produces retrieval of records having any or all of the *OR* terms. For example, the logical statement:

AUDIOLOGY ROOMS *OR* SOUND LEVEL

will retrieve documents which have one or more of these terms. The use of the *OR* operator broadens the search, reduces the coordination level and tends to increase recall.

The *AND* operator causes the retrieval of records where two or more terms or sets of terms co-occur in the same record. For example, the logical statement:

AUDIOLOGY ROOMS *AND* SOUND LEVEL

will retrieve only those records containing both terms. The *AND* operator narrows the search, increases the coordination level and improves precision.

The *NOT* operator prevents the retrieval of records indexed by a specific term. For example, the logical statement:

AUDIOLOGY ROOMS *NOT* SOUND LEVEL

will exclude those documents which have the term 'Sound level'.

The *NOT* operator should be used with care, as it is easy to eliminate relevant documents as well as the irrelevant. The *NOT* operator is particularly useful in non-subject searching (for example, language and form of document) to further refine a search. For example:

NOT GERMAN LANGUAGE
NOT THESIS

G2.2. Word fragment searching

A search may be broadened by searching on word fragments. This device is particularly useful when searching in natural language, but it is also applicable with controlled language.

Word fragment searching may use *right truncation*. For instance, all terms beginning with the stem AUDIO?

Or it may use *left truncation*. For example, all words ending with the stem ?OLOGY

Or it may use *infix truncation*, which retrieves words for which the beginning and end are specified but the middle is not. For example, P?DIATRICS will retrieve Pediatrics and Paediatrics.

Or the search may be made for a word fragment from any part of the term. For example, ?ELECTRIC? will retrieve Piezoelectric, Electricity, Electrical conductivity, etc. (the last case will depend, of course, on the computer having been instructed to treat Electrical conductivity as a compound term).

Truncation, while increasing recall, may retrieve many non-relevant items: the shorter the stem, the greater the possibility of ambiguity. In natural language searching, especially in science and technology databases, a type of thesaurus entry may be built up at the search stage by grouping word fragments, which will retrieve related terms. Lancaster (46, Chapter 17) shows how 'the ability to search on the suffixes 'biotics or illin or mycin or cycline or myxin' goes a long way toward equivalency with a conventional thesaurus entry 'antibiotics' that leads to a list of narrower antibiotic terms'.

G2.3. Word distance device

This device allows for retrieving terms which appear within a specified distance from each other. The range of proximity specifications includes adjacent words.

Example:

AUDIOLOGY (W) ROOMS   The terms are to be adjacent in the order given.

It also includes words within the range of one or more words.

Example:

AUDIOLOGY (nW) ROOMS   The terms are to appear within up to n intervening words in the order given.

Other possibilities are that the terms are to appear in any order and in any subfield of the same field.

This device improves precision and reduces false drops. Compound terms in controlled language perform a precision improvement role similar to that of the adjacent term device.

G3. Links

This device, used in post-coordinate systems to avoid false drops, is applied at both the indexing and searching stages. Links are used to show which terms are related in the same document, so that inappropriate combinations of terms are not retrieved. For example, a document number 1000 on 'Welding of copper pipes and heat treatment of steel structures' would be indexed:

WELDING	1000A
COPPER	1000A
PIPES	1000A
HEAT TREATMENT	1000B
STEEL	1000B
STRUCTURES	1000B

where the letters A and B indicate which terms are associated, thus ensuring that the document is not retrieved in a search for 'Welding of steel'.

Links are powerful devices, but can be detrimental to recall. The linkage may eliminate true as well as false combinations. For example, when links are used with different hierarchical levels:

LEAD   COATINGS   for   COPPER   PIPES
1000A   1000A   1000B   1000B

the false combination 'Copper coatings for lead pipes' is avoided, but the legitimate 'Coatings for pipes' is also excluded. The use of compound terms, for example, 'Lead coatings' and 'Copper pipes' serves the same purpose as links in the avoidance of false drops. The *API thesaurus* (75) is an example of a thesaurus employing links. Links add to indexing costs and need to be used with caution.

G4. Roles

The role indicator is a signal attached to the index term at the indexing stage to indicate the sense and use of the term in a particular context. It may be shown that a term is functioning as a 'Raw material', 'End product' or 'Component', or that it is 'passively receiving an operation' or functioning as an 'Agent' or 'Tool'.

The role indicator is most useful in avoiding recall of terms with incorrect function, particularly in chemical or nuclear processes. For instance, roles may be added to 'Nuclear particles' to distinguish between their functions as 'Projectiles' and as 'Products' in nuclear reactions:

Document	Index terms
Gamma neutron reaction (γn)	Reaction. Gamma (2). Neutron (3)
Neutron gamma reaction (nγ)	Reaction. Neutron (2). Gamma (3)

Roles: (2) Projectile, (3) Product

A set of role indicators produced by the Engineers Joint Council (EJC) is shown in Figure 4. Compilers of retrieval languages may develop their own roles, for example, the *API thesaurus* (75), although the EJC table

Figure 4. EJC role indicators

0 — Adjectives / Bibliographic Terms
- Authors, Both Personal and Corporate
- Types of Documents
- Journals -- Names, Month, Year, Volume Number, Issue Number (As Five Separate Terms)
- Language Of Original Document (If Foreign)
- All Adjectives

1 — Input Or Raw Material
- Reactant
- Base Metal Being Alloyed
- Components, Constituents, Or Ingredients Being Combined
- Materials Being Shaped Or formed
- Materials of Construction
- Components Being Assembled

2 — Output Or Product
- Products and Byproducts
- Alloys Produced By Designated Name
- Mixture Or Formulation Produced
- Forms or Shapes Being Made
- Structures Built Or Erected
- Devices Resulting From Assembling

3 — Undesirables
- Contaminants
- Impurities
- Pollutants
- Poisons
- Adulterants
- Undesirable Components

  { In Inputs / In Outputs / In Media or Environments / In Materials Used / In Materials Passively Receiving Actions }

4 — Indicated Uses
- To Be Used For --
- To Be Used As --
- For Use With --
- For Later Use In --
- To Be Used On --
- For Later Use As --

5 — Materials "In Which"
- In A -- Solvent
- In A -- Medium
- In -- As A Vehicle
- In An Atmosphere Of --
- In -- As A Carrier Gas
- In -- As The Dispersion Means

6 — That Which Affects / 7 — That Which Is Affected

Examples
(A) The Document Discusses The Effect Of (6) ----- On (7) -----.
(B) How (6) ----- Influences (7) ----- Is Discussed.
(C) The Document Discusses How (7) ----- Is Affected By (6)
(D) How (7) ----- Depends On (6) ----- Is Considered.

8 — Primary Topics Of Discussion
- -- Is Discussed
- -- Is Reported
- -- Is Described
- -- Is Considered
- The Topic Of Discussion Is --
- The Subject Of Consideration Is --

9 — Passive Recipients / Possessive (Possessors) / Location (Place And Time)
- Passive Recipients -- Terms for both concrete and abstract concepts which receive operations or processes but which are unchanged by the action
- Possessive (Possessors) -- Objects of the preposition "of", meaning possession, and other possessive forms.
- Location (Place And Time)-- Objects of the prepositions "in", "on", or "at", and other forms meaning location of place or in time; also objects of preposition, "within".

10 — Means Used
- Using --
- By Means Of --
- By --
- With -- (Meaning "Using")
- In Or On -- (Meaning "Using")
- Through -- (Meaning "Using")

provides a useful checklist. The example given below illustrates the use of EJC-type roles in a practical situation.

Example:

Document: 'Testing of the electric strength of oil impregnated cable paper by means of switching surges'

Roles

8	(Primary topic)	Testing
9	(Passively receiving an operation)	Oil impregnated paper
9	(Passively receiving an operation)	Electric strength
10	(Means to accomplish operation)	Switching surges

The use of roles here, for example, would effectively prevent the recall of this document in response to a search in which switching surges are considered the major topic.

As with links, roles are precision devices which, except in certain subject areas, are likely to be detrimental to recall. The reasons for this are clear:

It is difficult for indexers to apply the roles consistently.

It is even more difficult for the searcher to match the use of a role by the indexer. For instance, in the example above the searcher might consider 'Electric strength' as the main topic and code it 8. 'Oil impregnated cable paper' could be coded as role 5 'Environment', or as role 1 'Input' or 'Raw material'.

But it is not only the ambiguity of the roles that complicates searching, it is also the fact that the searcher is in ignorance of the interrelationship of terms in the indexing, when roles may be affected by the existence of unknown terms not featured in the terms of the questions.

Roles can be simulated to some extent by use of pre-coordinated terms. For example, the use of compound terms:

Gamma projectiles
Gamma product

is just as effective as using Gamma (Role 2) and Gamma (Role 3) to differentiate between the function of the particle as projectile and the particle as product, within a nuclear reaction.

Since roles are likely to curtail recall, and are at the same time expensive to operate at both the search and indexing stage of an information retrieval system, they are not cost-effective except in some specialized subject fields, such as Petroleum Technology. The *API thesaurus* (75) uses roles as well as links, which are described in an article by Hack (37).

G5. Treatment and other aspect codes

The precision performance may be improved by searching on terms, subheadings or equivalent codes added in a separate field at the time of indexing, which specify the treatment and other aspects of the document. For example, the treatment may be 'Practical', 'Experimental', 'Theoretical', or be concerned with 'New developments'. Similarly, it is possible to specify such aspects as the intended audience for the document, the language or physical form, or the subject bias of the document, such as Diagnosis or Side effects in a medical database.

G6. Weighting

In weighting systems, values are allocated to indexing terms or search terms according to their importance in particular documents or search programs. Weighting acts as a precision device and also as an output ranking device.

Figure 5 shows an early system of weights worked out by Maron and others.

Figure 5. Weights (Maron)

Weight	Description	When used
8/8	Major subject	The term is highly specific and covers an entire major subject of the document.
7/8	Major subject	The term is specific and covers most of a major subject of the document.
6/8	More generic subject	The term is too broad and covers a major subject.
5/8	Other important terms	Terms that would be used in a binary indexing system but not a major subject.
4/8	Less generic subject	The term relates to, but is too narrow to cover, a major subject.
3/8	Minor subject	Includes such terms as relate to results of experiments, intermediate methods, possible uses, etc.
2/8	Other subjects	Other relevant tags.
1/8	Barely relevant	Subjects classifier would not want to use, but feels that some users might consider relevant.

A less complex weighting system was used by the second Cranfield Project (17):

    9/10 For concepts in the main theme of the document
    7/8 For concepts in a major subsidiary theme
    5/6 For concepts in a minor subsidiary theme

Pre-coordinate weights are those added to the document at the indexing stage. For example, using weights, a document 'Low temperature silicon epitaxy' might be indexed as follows:

    9. Low temperature
    9. Silicon
   10. Epitaxial growth
    8. Substrates
    7. Films
    8. Vapour deposition
    8. Crystal growth
    6. Mercury vapour lamps

In this document mercury vapour lamps are used to illuminate the substrates during deposition; therefore Mercury vapour lamps is a minor concept. It would not be retrieved in response to a search for Mercury vapour lamps as a major concept, weighted more than 6. If all documents on 'Mercury vapour lamps' were required, the weights could be ignored. Term weights in individual documents may also be derived statistically, from within-document frequencies (19).

Pre-coordinate weighting systems are mainly restricted to research projects, but some operational systems offer a post-coordinate weighting facility.

In post-coordinate weighting, values are assigned to the search terms, reflecting their relative importance to the query. A document score is calculated from the sum of the weights of the matching terms. The output is then ranked in order of the document score. This procedure may be varied, for example, by weighting groups of terms and ranking the output according to the document score calculated on the sum of the matching-group weights. Weighting of search terms may also be a guide when adjusting search strategies. For instance, when reducing the coordination level, terms with lower weights may be excluded first, in the expectation that this will give optimum recall improvement.

Section H Thesaurus display

There are four basic types of thesaurus display:

(a) Alphabetical display with scope notes and showing equivalence, hierarchical and associative relationships under each indexing term. It may or may not have supporting systematic or graphic displays.

(b) Machine-generated hierarchies from the alphabetical display.

(c) Systematic display, supplemented by an alphabetical index or full alphabetical thesaurus.

(d) Graphic display, with an alphabetical index or full alphabetical thesaurus.

H1. Alphabetical display

H1.1. Layout and reference structure
The conventional form of the alphabetical display became established in 1967 on the publication of the *Thesaurus of engineering and scientific terms (TEST)* (101). (See Figure 6.) Preferred and non-preferred indexing terms are listed in one sequence in the following order:

PREFERRED TERM:
    SN   Scope notes or definitions
    UF   References to equivalent non-preferred terms
    BT   References to broader terms
    NT   References to narrower terms
    RT   References to related terms

Non-preferred term:
  USE PREFERRED TERM
      or

Non-preferred term
  USE PREFERRED TERM 1
    and PREFERRED TERM 2

Example:

Preferred term entry
  DEPRIVED FAMILIES
    SN   Socially disadvantaged and underprivileged
    UF   Underprivileged families
    BT   Families
    NT   Homeless families
        One-parent families
    RT   Deprivation

Non-preferred term entry

  Underprivileged families
    USE DEPRIVED FAMILIES

Figure 6. Conventional alphabetical display
Thesaurus of engineering and scientific terms (TEST)

—Food services
Cooking devices 0608
UF Electrical cooking devices
　　French fryers
　　Pressure cookers
　　Toasters
　　Waffle irons
RT Kitchen equipment and supplies
　　Kitchens
Cooking liquors (pulping) 1112
NT Spent sulfite liquors
　　Sulfite cooking liquors
　　White liquors
RT —Chemical pulping
　　Semichemical pulping
　—Spent liquors (pulping)
Cook off 2102
RT Propellant storage
　—Solid rocket propellants
Coolant pumps 1311
BT Pumps
RT —Air conditioning equipment
　　Cooling systems
　—Refrigerating machinery
Coolants 1301 1107
RT Air conditioning
　　Air cooling
　—Brines
　—Coolers
　—Cooling
　　Cooling systems
　　Cutting fluids
　　Dry ice®
　　Gas cooling
　—Liquid cooling
　　Liquid metal coolants
　　Nuclear reactor coolants
　—Nuclear reactors
　　Refrigerants
　　Water cooling
Coolers 1301
UF Aftercoolers
　　Intercoolers
　　Precoolers
NT Air coolers
　　Beverage coolers
　　Milk coolers
　　Oil coolers
　　Unit coolers
　　Water coolers
RT —Air conditioners
　—Air conditioning equipment
　—Compressors
　　Coolants
　—Cooling
　　Cooling systems
　　Dehumidifiers
　　Freezers
　　Ice refrigeration
　—Refrigerating
　—Refrigerating machinery
　—Refrigerators
Cool flames 2102
BT Flames
RT —Combustion
Cooling 1301 2013
UF Chilling
　　Heat dissipation
NT Adiabatic demagnetization
　　Air cooling
　—Evaporative cooling
　　Expansion cooling
　　Film cooling
　—Liquid cooling
　　Radiant cooling
　　Sublimation cooling
　　Sweat cooling

Thermoelectric cooling
　　Water cooling
RT Ablation
　　Air conditioning
　　Cold treatment
　—Condensing
　　Contraction
　　Coolants
　—Coolers
　—Cooling coils
　　Cooling curves
　　Cooling load
　　Cooling rate
　　Cooling systems
　　Cooling towers
　　Desuperheating
　　Environmental engineering
　—Fans
　　Flooding
　—Freezing
　—Heating
　　Heat loss
　　Heat radiators
　—Heat transfer
　　Hilsch tubes
　　Jackets
　—Melting
　—Quenching (cooling)
　　Recalescence
　—Refrigerating
　　Supercooling
　—Temperature
　　Temperature control
　　Temperature distribution
　　Thermal cycling tests
　　Thermal shock
　　Thermal stresses
　—Ventilation
　　Venting
　　Wetting
Cooling coils 1301
NT Direct expansion cooling coils
RT —Air conditioning equipment
　—Condensers (liquefiers)
　　Condenser tubes
　—Cooling
　　Cooling systems
　　Evaporators
　　Expansion valves
　　Gas expanders
　—Refrigerating machinery
Cooling curves 1301
BT Charts
　　Graphs (charts)
RT —Cooling
　　Cooling rate
　　Phase diagrams
　—Thermal analysis
Cooling fans 1301
BT Fans
Cooling fins 1301
UF †Finned tubes
　　Fins (coolers)
BT Fins
RT Cooling systems
　　Engine blocks
　　Engine cylinders
　　Heat exchangers
　　Heat radiators
Cooling load 1301
RT Air conditioning
　—Cooling
　　Enthalpy
　　Fluid infiltration
　　Heating load
　　Heat storage
　—Heat transfer
　　Heat transmission

　—Loads (forces)
　—Thermal insulation
Cooling rate 1301
BT Rates (per time)
RT Air conditioning
　—Cooling
　　Cooling curves
　　Cooling systems
　—Freezing
　—Precipitation heat treatment
　—Refrigerating
　　Thermal shock
　　Thermal stresses
Cooling systems 1301
UF Water cooling systems
RT Absorbers (equipment)
　　Absorption refrigeration
　　Air circulation
　—Air conditioners
　　Air conditioning
　—Air conditioning equipment
　　Air cooling
　　Beverage coolers
　　Blowers
　—Compressors
　—Condensers (liquefiers)
　　Coolant pumps
　　Coolants
　—Coolers
　—Cooling
　—Cooling coils
　　Cooling fins
　　Cooling rate
　　Cooling towers
　　Dehumidification
　　Ducts
　　Engine blocks
　—Evaporative cooling
　　Evaporators
　—Exhaust systems
　—Fans
　　Gas expanders
　　Heat exchangers
　　Heat pumps
　　Heat radiators
　　Heat sinks
　　Humidity control
　—Intake systems
　—Liquid cooling
　　Lubrication systems
　　Mechanical refrigeration
　　Piping systems
　—Porous metals
　　Refrigerants
　—Refrigerating
　—Refrigerating machinery
　　Registers (air circulation)
　　Steam jet apparatus
　　Steam jet refrigeration
　　Temperature control
　　Thermoelectric refrigeration
　—Transpiration
　　Transport refrigeration
　　Unit coolers
　—Ventilation
　　Vents
　　Water coolers
　　Water cooling
Cooling towers 1301 0701 1309
UF Water cooling towers
RT —Air conditioning equipment
　　Columns (process engineering)
　—Cooling
　　Cooling systems
　—Evaporative cooling
　—Refrigerating machinery
　　Water conservation
　　Water coolers

Subject Category Index numbers follow main terms; (—) = See main entry for narrower terms; † = Consult main entry;

Non-preferred term entry to terms to be used in combination to represent the concept (see also 'Syntactical factoring' in E2.4.2.a.)

One-parent family welfare
   USE ONE-PARENT FAMILIES
   and SOCIAL WELFARE

with access points under the constituent preferred terms

ONE-PARENT FAMILIES
   and SOCIAL WELFARE
   UF One-parent family welfare

SOCIAL WELFARE
   and ONE PARENT FAMILIES
   UF One-parent family welfare

International symbols are used in some thesauri:

Preferred term

= Equivalent terms, non-preferred
< Broader terms
> Narrower terms
− Related terms

Non-preferred terms

→ Preferred terms

A slightly modified version of these is used in the British Standards Institution *ROOT thesaurus* (81).

H1.2. Multilevel hierarchies

The conventional alphabetical thesaurus does not show the full hierarchy of broader and narrower terms at the entry point for the indexing term. The information given is at only one hierarchical step above and below the term.

Some thesauri, for example the *CAB thesaurus* (83) shown in Figure 7 and the European Community's *Food: multilingual thesaurus* (85) give broader and narrower terms to more than one level in the main alphabetical display, for example:

DEPRIVED FAMILIES
   UF   Underprivileged families
   BT1   Families
     BT2   Social institutions
   NT1   Homeless families
   NT1   One-parent families
     NT2   Fatherless families
   RT   Deprivation

Other thesauri show multilevel hierarchies inherent within the structure of the alphabetical thesaurus by computer-derived hierarchical displays, which are printed in a sequence separated from the main alphabetical section (see H2).

H1.3. Permuted index

In computerized thesauri a separate index may be prepared to bring to the front the second and third words in compound terms. This index is especially useful in making accessible constituent terms which are not indexing terms and therefore do not occur anywhere else in the

Figure 7. Multi-level alphabetical thesaurus
CAB thesaurus

DOMESTIC PRODUCTION (C)
  rt   self sufficiency

domestic science
  USE **home economics**

DOMESTIC TRADE
  uf   *trade, domestic*
  BT1   trade

DOMESTICATED BIRDS
  BT1   birds
  NT1   pigeons
  NT1   poultry
  NT2   capons
  NT2   chickens
  NT3   bantams
  NT3   broilers
  NT3   chicks
   NT4   day old chicks
  NT3   cockerels
  NT3   pullets
  NT2   drakes
  NT2   ducks
  NT3   ducklings
  NT3   wild ducks
  NT2   geese
  NT3   ganders
  NT3   goslings
  NT2   guinea fowl
  NT2   hens
  NT2   turkeys
  NT3   poults
  NT3   toms
  rt   domestic animals
  rt   poultry

DOMESTICATION
  uf   *speciation*
  rt   crops
  rt   domestic animals
  rt   evolution

DOMIATI CHEESE
  BT1   cheeses
  BT2   milk products
  BT3   dairy products
  BT4   products
  BT3   livestock products

DOMINANCE
  NT1   apical dominance
  NT1   codominance
  NT1   epistatic deviation
  NT1   overdominance
  NT1   semidominance
  rt   alleles
  rt   dominant genes
  rt   dominant lethals
  rt   dominant species
  rt   ecological succession
  rt   genetics
  rt   overdominant genes

DOMINANT GENES
  BT1   genes
  rt   dominance

DOMINANT LETHALS
  uf   *lethals, dominant*
  BT1   lethals
  BT2   genes
  BT2   genetic defects
  BT3   abnormalities
  BT3   defects
  rt   dominance

DOMINANT SPECIES
  BT1   species
  rt   climax communities
  rt   competitive ability
  rt   dominance
  rt   multispecies fisheries
  rt   plant interaction
  rt   plant succession

DOMINICA
  BT1   caribbean
  BT2   america
  rt   acp
  rt   caribbean community
  rt   commonwealth of nations
  rt   windward islands

DOMINICAN REPUBLIC
  BT1   caribbean
  BT2   america
  BT1   central america
  rt   threshold countries

DON
  BT1   goat breeds
  BT2   breeds
  BT1   horse breeds

DONAX
  BT1   mollusca

DONGOLA
  BT1   horse breeds
  BT2   breeds

doob
  USE **cynodon dactylon**

DOOR TO DOOR SALES
  BT1   marketing techniques
  BT2   marketing
  BT2   techniques
  BT1   retail marketing
  BT2   marketing channels
  BT3   marketing

DOORS
  BT1   buildings
  rt   gates

DOPA
  uf   *3,4-dihydroxyphenylalanine*
  BT1   catecholamines
  BT2   ammonium compounds
  BT1   neurotransmitters
  BT1   phenylalanine
  BT2   essential amino acids
  BT3   amino acids
  BT1   sympatholytics
  BT2   neurotropic drugs
  NT1   aldomet
  rt   levodopa

DOPAMINE
  BT1   catecholamines
  BT2   ammonium compounds
  BT1   neurotransmitters
  NT1   bromocriptine
  rt   cholinergic mechanisms

DOPAMINE BETA-MONOOXYGENASE
  (ec 1.14.17.1)
  BT1   oxidoreductases
  BT2   enzymes

DOPATRIUM
  BT1   scrophulariaceae
  NT1   dopatrium junceum

DOPATRIUM JUNCEUM
  BT1   dopatrium
  BT2   scrophulariaceae

DOPING
  BT1   drug therapy
  BT2   therapy
  rt   depression
  rt   stimulation
  rt   varnishes

doralis
  USE **aphis**

doralis fabae
  USE **aphis fabae**

DORITIS
  BT1   orchidaceae
  NT1   doritis pulcherrima

DORITIS PULCHERRIMA
  BT1   doritis
  BT2   orchidaceae

DORITIS PURCHERRIMA
  BT1   ornamental plants

DORMANCY
  BT1   developmental stages
  BT2   development
  NT1   aestivation

DORMANCY (C)
  NT1   diapause
  NT1   seed dormancy
  NT1   torpor
  rt   biological rhythms
  rt   bud break
  rt   buds
  rt   dormancy breakers
  rt   germination
  rt   hard seeds
  rt   hibernation
  rt   rest
  rt   sleep
  rt   stratification
  rt   vernalization

DORMANCY BREAKERS
  BT1   growth regulators
  rt   biostimulators
  rt   dormancy
  rt   gibberellins

DORMANCY BREAKING
  rt   germination

DORONICUM
  BT1   compositae
  NT1   doronicum cordifolium
  NT1   doronicum macrophyllum
  NT1   doronicum oblongifolium

DORONICUM CORDIFOLIUM
  BT1   doronicum
  BT2   compositae
  BT1   ornamental plants

DORONICUM MACROPHYLLUM
  BT1   doronicum
  BT2   compositae
  BT1   medicinal plants

DORONICUM OBLONGIFOLIUM
  BT1   doronicum
  BT2   compositae
  BT1   medicinal plants

DOROSOMA
  BT1   clupeoidei
  BT1   fishes
  rt   shad

DOROTHEANTHUS BELLIDIFLORUS
  uf   *mesembryanthemum criniflorum*

DORPER
  BT1   sheep breeds
  BT2   breeds

DORSET DOWN
  BT1   sheep breeds
  BT2   breeds

DORSET HORN
  BT1   sheep breeds
  BT2   breeds

DORYALIS
  uf   *dovyalis*
  BT1   flacourtiaceae
  NT1   doryalis caffra

DORYALIS CAFFRA
  uf   *dovyalis caffra*
  BT1   doryalis
  BT2   flacourtiaceae
  BT1   tropical fruits

DORYANTHES
  BT1   amaryllidaceae

DORYLAIMIDAE
  NT1   enchodelus
  NT1   eudorylaimus

DORYLUS
  BT1   hymenoptera
  NT1   dorylus labiatus

DORYLUS LABIATUS
  BT1   dorylus
  BT2   hymenoptera

DORYPHORA
  BT1   atherospermataceae

thesaurus. The permuted index is usually in the form of a KWIC or KWOC index. Figure 8 shows an extract from the permuted index included in the *Political science thesaurus* (78). Where a separate permuted index is not published, it may be useful to add to the main alphabetical sequence lead-in terms from words in compound terms, which do not exist as preferred terms in the thesaurus. For example:

> Induction, electrostatic
> use ELECTROSTATIC INDUCTION

where the term 'Induction' is not an indexing term.

H1.4. Alphabetization
There are two main human systems of alphabetization: letter-by-letter or word-by-word. Once the decision has been made to accept either of these systems, the rules should be clearly stated in the introduction to the thesaurus. It may be necessary in computer systems to prepare special programs to meet either of these alternatives.

○ Letter-by-letter arrangement
In this system all spaces between words are ignored, as well as all characters other than left parenthesis, numbers and letters. Items are filed according to the sequence:

> Left parenthesis
> Numerals in ascending value
> Letters A–Z

This system brings together words which may be spelled as one word, two words, or hyphenated:

> Metalworking
> Metal working
> Metal-working

but on the other hand related terms may be separated in the sequence, as are the terms for lead compounds generally and specific lead compounds in the following example:

> Lead compounds
> Leadership
> Leading edges
> Lead oxide
> Lead selenide

○ Word-by-word arrangement
In this system, favoured by the British Standard on alphabetical arrangement, each word is considered in turn and a given complete word will precede any term beginning with the same sequence of letters as part of the word. Word-by-word arrangement leads to the grouping of related terms, but this does not happen consistently because the arbitrary separation or joining of words affects the sequence. The two systems of alphabetization are compared below:

Word-by-word	*Letter-by-letter*
Black Arts	Black Arts
Black Book	Blackberry
Black Earth	Black Book
Blackberry	Blackburn
Blackburn	Black Earth

Hyphens are usually treated as spaces in alphabetization.

Figure 8. Permuted index
Political science thesaurus II

S	Civil Rights	Demonstrating
S-08-0015		Demonstration
S-08-0016	Civil Rights	Demonstration
S-08-0010	Consumer	Demonstration
S-08-0009	Economic	Demonstration
S-08-0019	Peace	Demonstration
S	Producer	Demonstration
S-08-0020	Student	Demonstration
S-08-0022	Veterans	Demonstration
S-08-0023	Worker	Demonstration
S-32-0180		Demonstrator
S		Denationalization
S-31-0343		Denationalization Process
G-06-0018		Denmark
S		Denominational School
S-06-0364	Population	Density
S-36-0006		Department Head
S	Academic	Departments
S-06-0621	Economic	Dependency
S-16-0118		Dependent Nation
S-24-0427		Dependent Variable
S-12-0017		Depressed Area
S-12-0016		Depressed Economy
S-31-0137		Depression
S-06-0281	Economic	Depression
S-06-0126		Deprivation
S-06-0622	Economic	Deprivation
S-06-0127	Relative	Deprivation
S-38-0551	Relative	Deprivation Theory
S-38-0549	Psychological	Deprogramming
S-24-0108		Depth Interview
S-31-0346	Government	Deregulation
S-31-0345		Deregulation Process
S-04-0004		Derived Authority
S-06-0789	Objectively	Derived Status
S-06-0790	Subjectively	Derived Status
S-20-0003	Bilateral Family	Descent Pattern
S-20-0002	Family	Descent Pattern
S-20-0004	Matrilineal Family	Descent Pattern
S-20-0005	Patrilineal Family	Descent Pattern
S-24-0382		Descriptive Research
S-24-0065		Descriptive Statistics
S-26-0382		Desegregation Policy
S-26-0383	Community	Desegregation Policy
S-26-0384	School	Desegregation Policy
S-10-0059		Desertion
S	Building	Design
S-24-0370	Most Different System	Design
S-24-0371	Most Similar System	Design
S-24-0340	Research	Design
S-31-0670	Urban	Design
S-06-0716	Socially	Desirable Behavior
S-31-0479	Cease	Desist Order
S-32-0221		Despot
S-32-0222	Benevolent	Despot
S-32-0223	Oriental	Despot

Figure 9. Machine-generated hierarchies
INSPEC thesaurus

Hierarchies

terrestrial atmosphere - cont.

. atmospheric precipitation
. . rain
. . snow
. atmospheric pressure and density
. atmospheric radiation
. atmospheric radioactivity
. . fallout
. atmospheric spectra
. atmospheric structure
. atmospheric techniques
. . ionospheric techniques
. atmospheric temperature
. atmospheric thermodynamics
. atmospherics
. clouds
. fog
. stratosphere
. . ozonosphere
. troposphere
. . atmospheric boundary layer
. upper atmosphere
. . airglow
. . . nightglow
. . atmospheric elementary particle precipitation
. . . atmospheric electron precipitation
. . . atmospheric proton precipitation
. . aurora
. . exosphere
. . ionosphere
. . . D-region
. . . E-region
. . . . sporadic-E layer
. . . F-region
. . magnetosphere
. . . radiation belts
. . mesosphere
. . thermosphere

test equipment
. automatic test equipment
. battery testers

testing
. automatic testing
. computer testing
. electron device testing
. . electron tube testing
. . semiconductor device testing
. electronic equipment testing
. . computer equipment testing
. . printed circuit testing
. environmental testing
. impulse testing
. insulation testing
. integrated circuit testing
. life testing
. logic testing
. machine testing
. materials testing
. . corrosion testing
. . creep testing
. . dynamic testing
. . . fatigue testing
. . fracture toughness testing
. . hardness testing

Top term entry to hierarchies

automatic telephone systems
BT telephone systems
TT telecommunication systems
RT electronic switching systems
    telephone equipment
    telephony
CC B6210D C3370C
DI January 1973

automatic teller machines
BT EFTS
TT computer applications
RT bank data processing
    banking
    point of sale systems
DI January 1985
PT electronic funds transfer systems
    point of sale systems

automatic test equipment
UF computerised test equipment
BT computerised instrumentation
    test equipment
TT computer applications
    test equipment
RT automatic testing
    logic analysers
    quality control
    reliability
    testing
CC B7210B C3200 C3380B C7400
DI January 1973

automatic testing
UF built-in testing
    self testing
BT testing
TT testing
RT automatic test equipment
    quality control
    reliability
CC B7210B C3380
DI January 1973

automation, social aspects
    USE social aspects of automation

automobile electronics
    USE automobiles

automobile industry
UF motor industry
BT industries
TT industries
RT automobiles
DI January 1973

automobiles
UF automobile electronics
    cars (vehicles)
BT road vehicles
TT vehicles
RT automobile industry
    road traffic
CC B8520 B8520B B8620 C3360B C3350Z
DI January 1973

H2. Machine-generated hierarchies

These are hierarchical displays generated by computer from the one-level broader/narrower term data existing in the alphabetical thesaurus. They complement the alphabetical thesaurus by displaying preferred terms in the context of their full hierarchy (see also H1.2).

H2.1. Top term arrangement

In this type of hierarchical display, developed for the *INSPEC thesaurus* (Figure 9), the top terms (TTs) of the hierarchy are listed in a separate alphabetical sequence, each followed by the full sequence of subordinate terms. Indexing terms are located within these hierarchies via entries in the alphabetical display showing the top term of the hierarchy to which the term belongs.

Example in the style of the *INSPEC thesaurus:*

> *Alphabetical section*
> One-parent families
>   BT   Deprived families
>   NT   Fatherless families
>   TT   Social institutions
>
> *Machine-generated hierarchies*
> Social institutions
>
>   …
>   Families
>   .Deprived families
>   . . Homeless families
> →. . One-parent families
>   . . . Fatherless families

H2.2. Two-way hierarchies

Another way of showing multilevel hierarchies is found in the two-way hierarchies style of the *Thesaurus of ERIC descriptors* (102) illustrated in Figure 10, where the broader and narrower terms of the indexing term are given above and below the preferred term in indented positions.

Example:

. Social institutions	(Broader term 1)
Families	(Preferred term)
. Deprived families	(Narrower term level 1)
. . Homeless families	(Narrower term level 2)
. . One-parent families	(Narrower term level 2)
. . . Fatherless families	(Narrower term level 3)

The preferred terms are arranged in alphabetical sequence.

Figure 10. Machine-generated hierarchies
Thesaurus of ERIC descriptors
Two-way hierarchical term display

```
:::IDENTIFICATION            :LANGUAGES                  ::LANGUAGES
::EDUCATIONAL DIAGNOSIS      MODERN LANGUAGES            :AFRICAN LANGUAGES
:READING DIAGNOSIS                                      MOSSI
MISCUE ANALYSIS
                             ::CURRICULUM
                             :MATHEMATICS CURRICULUM     ::ATTITUDES
MNEMONICS                    MODERN MATHEMATICS          :PARENT ATTITUDES
                                                        MOTHER ATTITUDES

:::FACILITIES                ::DESIGN
::EDUCATIONAL FACILITIES     :BUILDING DESIGN            :::GROUPS
:CLASSROOMS                  MODULAR BUILDING DESIGN     ::FAMILY (SOCIOLOGICAL
MOBILE CLASSROOMS                                          UNIT)
                                                        :ONE PARENT FAMILY
                             MOLECULAR STRUCTURE         MOTHERLESS FAMILY
:CLINICS
MOBILE CLINICS
                             MONETARY SYSTEMS            ::GROUPS
                                                        :PARENTS
::::SERVICES                                            ::GROUPS
:::HUMAN SERVICES                                       :FEMALES
::SOCIAL SERVICES            ::GOVERNANCE               MOTHERS
:ANCILLARY SCHOOL SERVICES   :ADMINISTRATION            .BLACK MOTHERS
MOBILE EDUCATIONAL SERVICES  MONEY MANAGEMENT           .UNWED MOTHERS

                             :::LANGUAGES
::FACILITIES                 ::URALIC ALTAIC LANGUAGES   :LITERARY DEVICES
:LABORATORIES                :MONGOLIAN LANGUAGES        MOTIFS
MOBILE LABORATORIES          MONGOLIAN

                                                        :SCIENTIFIC CONCEPTS
MOBILITY                     ::LANGUAGES                MOTION
 .EDUCATIONAL MOBILITY       :URALIC ALTAIC LANGUAGES
 .MIGRATION                  MONGOLIAN LANGUAGES
 ..FAMILY MOBILITY            .BURIAT                   MOTIVATION
 ..MIGRATION PATTERNS         .DAGUR                     .ACHIEVEMENT NEED
 ..RELOCATION                 .MONGOLIAN                 .LEARNING MOTIVATION
 ...RURAL RESETTLEMENT                                   .STUDENT MOTIVATION
 ..RURAL TO URBAN MIGRATION                             .TEACHER MOTIVATION
 ..STUDENT MOBILITY
 ..URBAN TO RURAL MIGRATION  MONOLINGUALISM
 ..URBAN TO SUBURBAN                                    :METHODS
   MIGRATION                                            MOTIVATION TECHNIQUES
 .OCCUPATIONAL MOBILITY      :LITERARY DEVICES
 ..CAREER LADDERS            MONOLOGS
 ..FACULTY MOBILITY                                     :::DEVELOPMENT
 ..TEACHER TRANSFER                                     ::INDIVIDUAL DEVELOPMENT
 .PHYSICAL MOBILITY          MORAL CRITICISM (1969 1980) :PHYSICAL DEVELOPMENT
 ..VISUALLY HANDICAPPED                                 MOTOR DEVELOPMENT
   MOBILITY
 .SOCIAL MOBILITY            ::DEVELOPMENT
                             :INDIVIDUAL DEVELOPMENT     ::BEHAVIOR
                             MORAL DEVELOPMENT           :RESPONSES
:EQUIPMENT                                              MOTOR REACTIONS
MOBILITY AIDS                                            .EYE MOVEMENTS
 .WHEELCHAIRS                :PSYCHOLOGICAL PATTERNS      ..EYE FIXATIONS
                             MORALE                       .PUPILLARY DILATION
                              .TEACHER MORALE
:BEHAVIOR
MODELING (PSYCHOLOGY)                                    :EQUIPMENT
                             MORAL ISSUES               MOTOR VEHICLES
                                                         .SERVICE VEHICLES
::METHODS                                                ..BOOKMOBILES
:SIMULATION                  :VALUES                      ..SCHOOL BUSES
MODELS                       MORAL VALUES                .TRACTORS
 .MATHEMATICAL MODELS
 .ROLE MODELS
 ..MENTORS                   ::::LINGUISTICS
 .STUDENT WRITING MODELS     :::DESCRIPTIVE LINGUISTICS  ::STRUCTURAL ELEMENTS
 .TEACHING MODELS            ::GRAMMAR                     (CONSTRUCTION)
                             :MORPHOLOGY (LANGUAGES)     :EQUIPMENT
                             MORPHEMES                   :SPACE DIVIDERS
::DISABILITIES                .NEGATIVE FORMS (LANGUAGE) MOVABLE PARTITIONS
:MENTAL RETARDATION           .PLURALS
MODERATE MENTAL RETARDATION   .SUFFIXES
```

H2.3. Medical Subject Headings (MeSH) tree structures

These are hierarchies of broader/narrower terms of up to seven levels. Terms within the same hierarchical level are ordered alphabetically. The hierarchies are allocated a notation, so that reference may be made to the broader/narrower term structure from the main alphabetical section of *Medical Subject Headings* (*MeSH*)(95), which contains 'see also' (related term) references but no hierarchical information. The hierarchies in the tree structures are arranged under broad headings (see Figure 11).

H3. Systematic displays

A systematic display (also known as a classified or subject display) 'arranges categories or hierarchies of terms according to their meanings and logical interrelationships'.

A systematic thesaurus must always have two parts:

○ The systematic section.

○ The alphabetical section. (Either an index or full thesaurus which directs the user to the appropriate parts of the systematic section.)

Thesauri differ in the emphasis each puts on the two sections. The systematic section may be an auxiliary if the main part of the thesaurus is the alphabetical; or it may be the main part of the thesaurus, carrying all definitional and relational data, with the alphabetical section in its index form playing a minor role; or the systematic section and alphabetical section may have equal status, the relational data being divided between them, or provided in full under both sections of the thesaurus.

The link between the two systems is usually the notation (i.e., an address code of numbers and letters – see F5), which is added to the systematic section and which functions as a reference in the alphabetical thesaurus.

A systematic display provides an 'overall structure or macro-classification' (ISO 2788) within which the relations between hierarchies (see F2) and groups of terms otherwise related (see F1 and F3) may be clarified and presented. The creation of systematic displays is discussed more fully at F4 and J7.2.1. There are several options to consider when developing this type of display, including:

○ Broad subject groups, versus detailed systems.

○ Facet classification, versus enumerative, non-facet systems.

○ Primary arrangement by discipline or subject field, versus by fundamental facets.

○ The systematic display as the source of the alphabetical display versus a separate classification having a different structure against which the indexing terms are arranged.

In this manual, systematic thesauri are grouped into three main categories: (1) broad subject groups, (2) enumerative-non-faceted classification and (3) detailed faceted classification.

Figure 11a. Machine-generated hierarchies
Medical Subject Headings – tree structures
(Codes in small type indicate location of terms in other hierarchies)

C11 – DISEASES–OCULAR

EYE DISEASES

EYE DISEASES	C11			
ALBINISM	C11.38	C17.621.102	C17.827.130	C18.452.648.
ASTHENOPIA	C11.83			
CONJUNCTIVAL DISEASES	C11.187			
CONJUNCTIVAL NEOPLASMS	C11.187.169	C4.588.364.	C11.319.217	
CONJUNCTIVITIS	C11.187.183			
CONJUNCTIVITIS, ALLERGIC	C11.187.183.200	C20.543.480.		
CONJUNCTIVITIS, BACTERIAL	C11.187.183.220	C1.252.230		
CONJUNCTIVITIS, INCLUSION	C11.187.183.220.180	C1.850.200.		
OPHTHALMIA NEONATORUM	C11.187.183.220.538	C1.252.391.	C16.614.677	
TRACHOMA	C11.187.183.220.889	C1.850.200.		
CONJUNCTIVITIS, VIRAL	C11.187.183.240	C2.190		
CONJUNCTIVITIS, ACUTE HEMORRHAGIC	C11.187.183.240.216	C2.190.216	C2.782.687.	
KERATOCONJUNCTIVITIS	C11.187.183.394	C11.204.564.		
KERATOCONJUNCTIVITIS, INFECTIOUS	C11.187.183.394.520	C1.252.480	C22.500	
KERATOCONJUNCTIVITIS SICCA ·	C11.187.183.394.550			
➡ REITER'S DISEASE	C11.187.183.749	C1.539.717 C20.111.782	C5.550.114.	C12.777.767.
PTERYGIUM	C11.187.781			
CORNEAL DISEASES	C11.204			
ARCUS SENILIS ·	C11.204.104			
CORNEAL DYSTROPHIES	C11.204.236			
FUCHS' ENDOTHELIAL DYSTROPHY ·	C11.204.236.438			
CORNEAL OPACITY	C11.204.299			
KERATITIS	C11.204.564			
CORNEAL ULCER	C11.204.564.225			
KERATITIS, DENDRITIC	C11.204.564.418	C2.256.466.		
KERATOCONJUNCTIVITIS	C11.204.564.585	C11.187.183.		
KERATOCONUS	C11.204.627			
SIDEROSIS	C11.204.855	C8.381.655.	C21.447.800.	
EXOPHTHALMOS	C11.280			
GOITER, EXOPHTHALMIC	C11.280.451	C19.874.283.	C19.874.397.	C20.111.540
EYE MANIFESTATIONS	C11.300	C23.888.357		
EYE NEOPLASMS	C11.319	C4.588.364		
CONJUNCTIVAL NEOPLASMS	C11.319.217	C4.588.364.	C11.187.169	
EYELID NEOPLASMS	C11.319.421	C4.588.364.	C11.338.526	
UVEAL NEOPLASMS	C11.319.494	C4.588.364.	C11.941.855	
CHOROID NEOPLASMS	C11.319.494.198	C4.588.364.	C11.941.855.	
EYELID DISEASES	C11.338			
BLEPHARITIS ·	C11.338.133			
BLEPHAROPTOSIS	C11.338.204			
BLEPHAROSPASM ·	C11.338.250			
ECTROPION	C11.338.362			
ENTROPION	C11.338.443			
EYELID NEOPLASMS	C11.338.526	C4.588.364.	C11.319.421	
HORDEOLUM	C11.338.648	C1.252.868.		
GLAUCOMA	C11.381			
GLAUCOMA, OPEN–ANGLE	C11.381.407			
HYDROPHTHALMOS	C11.381.477	C16.614.438		
HERPES ZOSTER, OCULAR	C11.419	C2.256.466.		
HYPHEMA	C11.453	C23.542.616		
LACRIMAL APPARATUS DISEASES	C11.496			
DACRYOCYSTITIS	C11.496.221			
LACRIMAL DUCT OBSTRUCTION	C11.496.456			
SJOGREN'S SYNDROME	C11.496.719	C5.550.114. C20.111.199.	C5.799.114. C23.205.200.	C7.465.815.

· INDICATES MINOR DESCRIPTOR

Figure 11b. Machine-generated hierarchies
Medical Subject Headings – annotated alphabetic list

REIMPLANTATION see REPLANTATION
E4.936.494 +

REIMPLANTATION, TOOTH see TOOTH REPLANTATION
E4.833.876   E4.936.494.711
E6.397.898   E6.892.876

REINDEER
B2.649.77.373.644 +
IM; when IM, only /anat /blood-csf-urine /class /embryol /genet /growth
/immunol /metab /microbiol /parasitol /physiol /surg
68
XU CARIBOU

REINFORCEMENT (PSYCHOLOGY)
F2.463.425.770 +
human & animal; no qualif; DF: REINFORCEMENT
65; was REINFORCEMENT LEARNING 1963-64
X   NEGATIVE REINFORCEMENT
X   POSITIVE REINFORCEMENT

REINFORCEMENT SCHEDULE
F2.463.425.770.644
human & animal; no qualif
69(66)

REINFORCEMENT, SOCIAL
F2.463.425.770.706
no qualif
69
X   SOCIAL REINFORCEMENT

REINFORCEMENT, VERBAL
F2.463.425.770.769
no qualif
69(66)

→ REITER'S DISEASE
C1.539.717   C5.550.114.782
C11.187.183.749   C12.777.767.851.644
C20.111.782
XR ERYTHEMA MULTIFORME

REJECTION (PSYCHOLOGY)
F1.145.76.850
no qualif; DF: REJECTION
75

REJUVENATION
E2.849
no qualif

RELAPSING FEVER
C1.252.847.193.644
a disease entity caused by Borrelia: not for 'recurrent fever' (= FEVER (IM)
+ RECURRENCE (NIM))

RELATIVE BIOLOGICAL EFFECTIVENESS
G3.850.810.250.275
NIM; no qualif
77

RELAXATION
I3.450.769 +
no qualif; note category; not for muscle relaxation (index MUSCLE
RELAXATION)

RELAXATION TECHNICS
F4.754.137.750
do not confuse with RELAXATION (I3); not for physiological relaxation of
muscles (= MUSCLE RELAXATION); SPEC qualif; transcendental
meditation goes here   CATALOG: do not use /laboratory manuals
76

RELAXIN
D6.472.866.362.769
/biosyn /physiol permitted

RELIEF WORK
G3.230.100.300
no qualif
(75); was see under DISASTERS & INDIGENT CARE 1963-67
search DISASTERS 1968-74 & DISASTERS & INDIGENT CARE 1966-67
see under DISASTERS

RELIGION
K1.844 +
only /hist; Saints: TN H
RELIGION AND SOCIOLOGY was heading 1963-65
X   RELIGIOUS BELIEFS
X   THEOLOGY

RELIGION AND MEDICINE
K1.844.619
no qualif; coord IM with medical aspect (IM)

RELIGION AND PSYCHOLOGY
F2.880 +   K1.844.664
no qualif; coord IM with psychol aspect (IM)

RELIGION AND SCIENCE
K1.844.709
no qualif; usually general; IM
XR SCIENCE

RELIGION AND SEX
K1.844.754
no qualif; coord IM with sexual aspect (IM)
XR SEX

RELIGIOUS BELIEFS see RELIGION
K1.844 +

RELIGIOUS PHILOSOPHIES (NON MESH)
K1.844.799 +
'religious philosophy' is indexed RELIGION + possibly PHILOSOPHY

REMANTADINE see RIMANTADINE
D2.219.75.700   D4.615.236.700
D20.388.815

REMEDIAL TEACHING
F2.784.629.709   I2.903.694
only /econ /methods /stand /trends

REMISSION, SPONTANEOUS
C23.280.775
NIM: never IM; no qualif; do not confuse with REGRESSION, a psychol
concept
(82); was REMISSION see under DISEASE 1975-81, was REMISSION
1971-74 (Prov)
use REMISSION, SPONTANEOUS to search REMISSION 1971-81 (as Prov
1971-74)
see under DISEASE

RENAL AGENTS (NON MESH)
D19.770 +
consider also DIURESIS /DE

RENAL ARTERY
A7.231.114.745
do not use /blood supply; thrombosis: index under RENAL ARTERY
OBSTRUCTION (IM) + THROMBOSIS (IM)

RENAL ARTERY OBSTRUCTION
C12.777.419.775   C14.907.137.727
obstruct of external or internal origin; renal artery thrombosis: coord IM with
THROMBOSIS (IM); consider also HYPERTENSION, RENOVASCULAR
(hypertension caused by renal artery obstruct or compress)
RENAL ARTERY STENOSIS was see under RENAL ARTERY
OBSTRUCTION 1963-83
use RENAL ARTERY OBSTRUCTION to search RENAL ARTERY
STENOSIS back thru 1966
X   RENAL ARTERY STENOSIS

RENAL ARTERY STENOSIS see RENAL ARTERY OBSTRUCTION
C12.777.419.775   C14.907.137.727

+ INDICATES THERE ARE INDENTED DESCRIPTORS IN MESH TREE STRUCTURES AT THIS NUMBER

Figure 12. Broad subject groups
Thesaurus of ERIC descriptors
Descriptor group display

TRADITIONAL GRAMMAR
TRANSFORMATIONAL GENERATIVE GRAMMAR
TRANSLATION
UNCOMMONLY TAUGHT LANGUAGES
UNWRITTEN LANGUAGE (1968 1980)
UNWRITTEN LANGUAGES
URBAN LANGUAGE
VERBAL ABILITY
VERBAL COMMUNICATION
VERBAL DEVELOPMENT
VERBS
VOCABULARY
VOCABULARY DEVELOPMENT
VOCABULARY SKILLS
VOWELS
WORD FREQUENCY
WRITTEN LANGUAGE

460 READING

ADULT LITERACY
ADULT READING PROGRAMS
BASAL READING
BASIC READING (1967 1980)
BEGINNING READING
CLOZE PROCEDURE
CONTENT AREA READING
CONTEXT CLUES
CORRECTIVE READING
CREATIVE READING (1966 1980)
CRITICAL READING
DECODING (READING)
DEVELOPMENTAL READING (1966 1980)
DIRECTED READING ACTIVITY
EARLY READING
ELECTIVE READING (1966 1980)
EYE VOICE SPAN
FACTUAL READING (1966 1980)
FUNCTIONAL LITERACY
FUNCTIONAL READING
GROUP READING (1966 1980)
ILLITERACY
INDEPENDENT READING
INDIVIDUAL READING (1966 1980)
INDIVIDUALIZED READING
INITIAL TEACHING ALPHABET
INTERPRETIVE READING (1966 1980)
LITERACY
LITERACY EDUCATION
MISCUE ANALYSIS
ORAL READING
PHONICS
PREREADING EXPERIENCE
READABILITY
READABILITY FORMULAS
READING
READING ABILITY
READING ACHIEVEMENT
READING ALOUD TO OTHERS
READING ASSIGNMENTS
READING ATTITUDES
READING CENTERS
READING COMPREHENSION
READING DEVELOPMENT (1966 1980)
READING DIAGNOSIS
READING DIFFICULTIES
READING DIFFICULTY (1966 1980)
READING FAILURE
READING GAMES
READING HABITS
READING IMPROVEMENT
READING INSTRUCTION
READING INTERESTS
READING LEVEL (1966 1980)
READING MATERIAL SELECTION
READING PROCESSES

470 PHYSICAL EDUCATION AND RECREATION

ARCHERY
ATHLETES
ATHLETIC COACHES
ATHLETIC FIELDS
ATHLETICS
BASEBALL
BASKETBALL
BICYCLING
CALISTHENICS
CAMPING
CHILDRENS GAMES
COMMUNITY RECREATION PROGRAMS
DAY CAMP PROGRAMS
EXERCISE
EXERCISE (PHYSIOLOGY) (1969 1980)
EXTRACURRICULAR ACTIVITIES
EXTRAMURAL ATHLETICS
FIELD HOCKEY
FOOTBALL
GAMES
GOLF
GYMNASTICS
HOBBIES
HORSEBACK RIDING
ICE SKATING
INTRAMURAL ATHLETICS
JOGGING
LACROSSE
LEISURE TIME
LIFETIME SPORTS
MOVEMENT EDUCATION
ORIENTEERING
OUTDOOR ACTIVITIES
PHYSICAL ACTIVITIES
PHYSICAL EDUCATION
PHYSICAL RECREATION PROGRAMS
PLAY
PLAYGROUND ACTIVITIES
RECREATION
RECREATIONAL ACTIVITIES
RECREATIONAL PROGRAMS
RECREATIONISTS
RESIDENT CAMP PROGRAMS
ROLLER SKATING
RUNNING
SCHOOL RECREATIONAL PROGRAMS
SKIING
SOCCER
SOFTBALL
SPORTSMANSHIP
SQUASH (GAME)
SWIMMING
TENNIS
TOYS
TRACK AND FIELD
TUMBLING
VOLLEYBALL
WATERSKIING
WEIGHTLIFTING
WOMENS ATHLETICS
WRESTLING

480 MATHEMATICS

ADDITION
ALGEBRA
ALGORITHMS
ANALYTIC GEOMETRY
ARITHMETIC
BAYESIAN STATISTICS
CALCULUS
COLLEGE MATHEMATICS
COMPUTATION

H3.1. Broad subject groups

In this type of layout the indexing terms are arranged in alphabetical order under appropriate broad subject groups or facets. The notation for the subject group is shown against the indexing term in the alphabetical section. This type of display is found in many thesauri in which the main emphasis is on the alphabetical section. Figure 12 shows an extract from the descriptor group display of *Thesaurus of ERIC descriptors* (102), and Figure 13 a page from the *UNESCO: IBE education thesaurus*'s faceted array of descriptors and identifiers (90).

H3.1.1. 'Themes'

This is a style of thesaurus developed by Jean Viet in France, which has been used in the layout of numerous thesauri for international organizations, mainly in the social sciences. Examples of such thesauri include the *Thesaurus for information processing in sociology* (107), the *International thesaurus of cultural development* (105), the *Thesaurus – mass communication* (108), and early editions of the *ILO thesaurus* (91). The systematic section is usually the main part of the thesaurus and consists of broad groups or facets, known as themes. The themes are subdivided first by named headings, and further by notated but unnamed subgroupings or clusters of terms of like meaning.

Within the subcategories and clusters, the indexing terms, preferred and non-preferred, are listed alphabetically, accompanied by scope notes, synonyms, and broader, narrower and related terms.

Access to the terms is by a KWIC or KWOC index. Figure 14 shows extracts from an early edition of the *EUDISED multilingual thesaurus for information processing in education* (104), prepared by Jean Viet for the Council of Europe's Educational Documentation and Information Committee. This edition was superseded in 1984 (109) by a thesaurus with a different layout consisting of an alphabetical section with multilevel hierarchies, a rotated index and graphic displays, described in H4.3 below.

In the United Nations–OECD *Macrothesaurus* (106), also edited by Viet, the roles of the systematic section and alphabetical section are reversed, and the relational detail is given under the indexing terms in the alphabetical section, which becomes the main part of the thesaurus (Figure 15). The systematic display, consisting of preferred terms only, listed under themes without additional data, is reduced to an auxiliary position. The *UNBIS thesaurus* (103) is very similar in layout, but retains scope notes and non-preferred terms in the systematic section.

H3.2. Enumerative, non-faceted classification

In this type of display the enumerative classification may be a separate classification, against which indexing terms are mapped or related in some way. The *INSPEC thesaurus* is one example of this (89).

In other thesauri, such as the Predicast thesauri (12), the enumerative classification forms a coding system, with the keywords functioning as an index to the codes.

It is possible to have a ROOT-style thesaurus (see H3.3.3), i.e., with the alphabetical display derived from the systematic display, when the systematic display is not fully-faceted, but semi-enumerative. An example is the *Martindale online drug information thesaurus* (98).

Figure 13. Broad subject groups
UNESCO: IBE education thesaurus
Faceted array of descriptors and identifiers

100 ABSTRACT IDEAS

CHILD WELFARE
EDUCATIONAL FUTUROLOGY
FREEDOM OF SPEECH
HUMAN DIGNITY
HUMAN RIGHTS
MORAL ISSUES
NEEDS
OPPORTUNITIES
POLITICAL ISSUES
PRODUCTIVE LIVING
PUBLIC SUPPORT
SOCIAL WELFARE
WELFARE
YOUTH OPPORTUNITIES
YOUTH WELFARE
　A FREEDOM OF ASSOCIATION

101 POLICIES

CITIZENSHIP
COLLECTIVISM
COLONIALISM
DEMOCRACY
DEVELOPED COUNTRIES
DEVELOPING COUNTRIES
INTERNATIONAL
　UNDERSTANDING
NATIONAL INTEGRATION
NATIONALISM
PATRIOTISM
POLICIES
POLITICAL THEORIES
RACISM
STATE CHURCH SEPARATION
WORLD PROBLEMS
　A FEMINISM

102 POLITICAL STRUCTURE

COMMUNITY
COMMUNITY CONTROL

COORDINATION
FEDERATIVE STRUCTURE
FOREIGN POLICY
GEOGRAPHIC REGIONS
GOVERNMENT
MUNICIPALITIES
POLICY MAKING
PROVINCIAL POWERS
VOTING
　A COMMUNITY ACTION

103 CENTRAL AGENCIES

AGENCIES
CENTRAL GOVERNMENT
GOVERNMENTAL STRUCTURE
INTERNATIONAL AGENCIES
REGIONAL AGENCIES
SOCIAL AGENCIES
WELFARE AGENCIES
YOUTH AGENCIES
　A ADULT EDUCATION
　　AGENCIES
　A COORDINATING AGENCIES

104 INTERMEDIATE, LOCAL
**　　AGENCIES**

CITY GOVERNMENT
COMMUNITY AGENCIES
　(PUBLIC)
LOCAL GOVERNMENT
PROVINCIAL AGENCIES
PROVINCIAL GOVERNMENT

105 AGENCY ROLE,
**　　RELATIONSHIP**

AGENCY ROLE
CENTRAL PROVINCIAL
　RELATIONSHIP
CITIZEN PARTICIPATION

Figure 14. Themes
EUDISED thesaurus

Descriptor group display

```
11200            PRE-SCHOOL EDUCATION. NURSERY SCHOOL
<CONT.>

EDUCATION IN THE HOME
    USE: HOME EDUCATION

HOME EDUCATION - EDUCATION A DOMICILE - HAUSERZIEHUNG
    UF: EDUCATION IN THE HOME
    BT: EDUCATION
    RT: HOMEBOUND

KINDERGARTEN
    USE: NURSERY SCHOOL

NURSERY SCHOOL - ECOLE MATERNELLE - KINDERGARTEN
    UF: KINDERGARTEN
    BT: PRIMARY SCHOOL

PRE-SCHOOL EDUCATION - EDUCATION PRE-SCOLAIRE -
                        VORSCHULERZIEHUNG
    BT: EDUCATION

11300            PRIMARY EDUCATION. SECONDARY EDUCATION.
                 HIGHER EDUCATION

11310    ELEMENTARY EDUCATION

            USE: PRIMARY EDUCATION

ELEMENTARY SCHOOL
    USE: PRIMARY SCHOOL

PRIMARY EDUCATION - ENSEIGNEMENT PRIMAIRE -
                    PRIMARBILDUNG
    UF: ELEMENTARY EDUCATION
    BT: SCHOOL SYSTEM
    RT: PRIMARY SCHOOL
        PUPIL

PRIMARY SCHOOL - ECOLE PRIMAIRE - PRIMARSCHULE
    UF: ELEMENTARY SCHOOL
    BT: SCHOOL
    NT: NURSERY SCHOOL
    RT: PRIMARY EDUCATION
        PUPIL
```

KWOC index

```
PRESENCE
    PRESENCE      19240
        USE: ATTENDANCE
PRESS
    PRESS         14240
PRESSURE
    PRESSURE GROUP      26440
PRESTIGE
    PRESTIGE      17673
PREVENTION
    PREVENTION    18640
PREVENTIVE
    PREVENTIVE MEDICINE   18640
PRICE
    PRICE         24230
PRIMARY
    PRIMARY EDUCATION   11310
    PRIMARY SCHOOL      11310
PRINCIPE
    SAN TOME AND PRINCIPE   3010C
PRINCIPLES
    PRINCIPLES OF EDUCATION   26100
PRINTING
    PRINTING      14210
PRIORITY
    PRIORITY      19210
PRISON
    PRISON        25650
    PRISON WELFARE      25650
PRISONER
    PRISONER      10360
PRIVATE
    PRIVATE EDUCATION   11130
    PRIVATE FUNDS       24340
    PRIVATE SCHOOL      11130
    PRIVATE TUTOR       20260
PRIZE
    PRIZE         17770
    PRIZE-GIVING        17770
PROBATION
    PROBATION     25650
    PROBATION OFFICER   20300
    PROBATION PERIOD    19410
    PROBATION SERVICE   25650
PROBATIONARY
    PROBATIONARY TEACHER   20240
PROBLEM
    PROBLEM CHILD       10350
    PROBLEM SOLVING     13430
```

Figure 15a. Themes
Macrothesaurus
Descriptor group display

01.
INTERNATIONAL COOPERATION.
INTERNATIONAL RELATIONS.

01.01
INTERNATIONAL COOPERATION.

01.01.01
DEVELOPMENT AID
DEVELOPMENT ASSISTANCE
   USE: DEVELOPMENT AID
FIRST DEVELOPMENT DECADE
FOREIGN AID
HORIZONTAL COOPERATION
INTERNATIONAL ASSISTANCE
   USE: INTERNATIONAL COOPERATION
INTERNATIONAL COOPERATION
REGIONAL COOPERATION
SECOND DEVELOPMENT DECADE
THIRD DEVELOPMENT DECADE

01.01.02
AID BY RELIGIOUS BODIES
   USE: PRIVATE AID
BILATERAL AID
MULTILATERAL AID
PRIVATE AID

01.01.03
AID IN KIND
CAPITAL AID
   USE: FINANCIAL AID
ECONOMIC AID
ECONOMIC ASSISTANCE
   USE: ECONOMIC AID
EXTERNAL FINANCING
FINANCIAL AID
FINANCIAL ASSISTANCE
   USE: FINANCIAL AID
FOOD AID
GRANTS IN KIND
   USE: AID IN KIND
HEALTH AID
TECHNICAL ASSISTANCE
   USE: TECHNICAL COOPERATION
TECHNICAL COOPERATION
TRAINING ASSISTANCE

01.01.04
AID COORDINATION
AID EVALUATION
AID FINANCING
AID PROGRAMMES
GRANTS
PROGRAMME EVALUATION
TERMS OF AID
TIED AID
   USE: TERMS OF AID

01.01.05
COUNTERPART
COUNTERPART FUNDS
COUNTERPART PERSONNEL

01.01.06
DEVELOPMENT PROJECTS
FEASIBILITY STUDIES
JOINT PROJECTS
MULTIPURPOSE PROJECTS

01.01.06 (cont.)
NEEDS ASSESSMENT
PILOT PROJECTS
PLANS OF OPERATION
   USE: PROJECT DOCUMENTS
PROJECT APPRAISAL
PROJECT DESIGN
PROJECT DOCUMENTS
PROJECT EVALUATION
PROJECT FINANCING
PROJECT IMPLEMENTATION
PROJECT MANAGEMENT
PROJECT MONITORING
   USE: PROJECT MANAGEMENT
PROJECT PLANNING
   USE: PROJECT DESIGN
PROJECT REQUEST
PROJECT REVISION
PROJECT SELECTION

01.01.07
AID AGENCIES
   USE: AID INSTITUTIONS
AID INSTITUTIONS
CONSULTANTS
DEVELOPMENT CENTRES
DEVELOPMENT PERSONNEL
EXPERTS

01.01.08
PEACE CORPS
VOLUNTARY SERVICES
VOLUNTEERS

01.02
INTERNATIONAL RELATIONS.

01.02.01
ALLIANCES
BILATERAL RELATIONS
BORDER INTEGRATION
COMMON MARKETS
COMPLEMENTARITY AGREEMENTS
ECONOMIC COOPERATION
ECONOMIC INTEGRATION
ECONOMIC INTERDEPENDENCE
ECONOMIC RELATIONS
FOREIGN RELATIONS
IMPERIALISM
INDUSTRIAL COOPERATION
INDUSTRIAL INTEGRATION
INTERNATIONAL AFFAIRS
   USE: INTERNATIONAL RELATIONS
INTERNATIONAL ECONOMIC RELATIONS
INTERNATIONAL POLITICS
INTERNATIONAL RELATIONS
INTERNATIONALIZATION
ISOLATIONISM
MILITARISM
MULTILATERAL RELATIONS
NEUTRALISM
NEUTRALITY
NEW INTERNATIONAL ECONOMIC ORDER
NON-ALIGNMENT
NORTH-SOUTH DIALOGUE
   USE: NORTH-SOUTH RELATIONS
NORTH-SOUTH RELATIONS
PROLETARIAN INTERNATIONALISM
REGIONAL INTEGRATION

01.02.02
→ ACCESS TO THE SEA
BORDERS
   USE: BOUNDARIES
BOUNDARIES
COASTAL AREAS
   USE: LITTORAL ZONES
EXCLUSIVE ECONOMIC ZONES
FRONTIERS
   USE: BOUNDARIES
TERRITORIAL SEA

01.02.03
AUTONOMY
   USE: INDEPENDENCE
COLONIAL COUNTRIES
COLONIES
   USE: COLONIAL COUNTRIES
DECOLONIZATION
ECONOMIC DEPENDENCE
INDEPENDENCE
SELF-DETERMINATION
TRUST TERRITORIES

01.02.04
CONVENTIONS
INTERNATIONAL AGREEMENTS
INTERNATIONAL CONTROL
INTERNATIONAL LAW
INTERNATIONAL NEGOTIATIONS
INTERNATIONAL SEA-BED AUTHORITY
LAW OF THE SEA
STATE LIABILITY
TREATIES
   USE: INTERNATIONAL AGREEMENTS

01.02.05
DIPLOMACY
FOREIGN INTERVENTION
FOREIGN POLICY
FOREIGN SERVICE

01.02.06
ARMAMENT
ARMED FORCES
ARMS EMBARGO
ARMS LIMITATION
   USE: DISARMAMENT
ARMS RACE
   USE: ARMAMENT
ARMY
   USE: ARMED FORCES
ATOMIC WEAPONS
   USE: NUCLEAR WEAPONS
BACTERIOLOGICAL WEAPONS
CONVENTIONAL WEAPONS
DEFENCE
DEFENCE POLICY
DISARMAMENT
MILITARY AID
MILITARY ASSISTANCE
   USE: MILITARY AID
MILITARY BASES
MILITARY EXPENDITURES
MILITARY PERSONNEL
MILITARY SERVICE
NUCLEAR DISARMAMENT
NUCLEAR WEAPONS
SOLDIERS
   USE: MILITARY PERSONNEL
WEAPON PROCUREMENT
WEAPONS

Figure 15b. Themes
Macrothesaurus
Alphabetical descriptor display

ABACA
ABACA / ABACA - 07.07.07
  UF: *MANILA HEMP*
  TT: FIBRES
         PRODUCTS
  BT: SOFT FIBRES
         TEXTILE FIBRES
  RT: HEMP

ABANDONED CHILDREN
ENFANTS ABANDONNES / NINOS
ABANDONADOS - 02.04.02
  TT: AGE GROUPS
  BT: CHILDREN
  RT: ORPHANAGES

ABBREVIATIONS
ABREVIATIONS / ABREVIATURAS - 19.02.07
  RT: INDEXING

ABILITY GROUPING
GROUPEMENT PAR APTITUDES /
AGRUPAMIENTO POR APTITUD - 06.04.10
  UF: *STREAMING*
  RT: CLASSES

ABORIGINAL POPULATION
  USE: INDIGENOUS POPULATION - 14.03.01

ABORTION
AVORTEMENT / ABORTO - 14.05.02
  NT: LEGAL ABORTION
  RT: PREGNANCY

ABRASIVES
ABRASIFS / ABRASIVOS - 08.12.08

ABSENTEEISM
ABSENTEISME / AUSENTISMO - 13.05.00
  RT: LEAVE OF ABSENCE

ABSORPTIVE CAPACITY
CAPACITE D'ABSORPTION / CAPACIDAD DE
ABSORCION - 11.02.06
  RT: DEVELOPMENT AID
         INVESTMENTS

ABSTRACTING SERVICES
  USE: BIBLIOGRAPHIC SERVICES - 19.01.03

ABSTRACTS
RESUMES / RESUMENES ANALITICOS - 19.02.07
  TT: DOCUMENTS
  BT: SECONDARY DOCUMENTS

ABUNDANCE
ABONDANCE / ABUNDANCIA - 03.02.05
  RT: AFFLUENT SOCIETY
         WEALTH

ACADEMIC FREEDOM
LIBERTE DE L'ENSEIGNEMENT / LIBERTAD
DE ENSENANZA - 04.02.02
  TT: FREEDOM
  BT: CIVIL LIBERTIES
  RT: EDUCATIONAL SYSTEMS

ACAST
CCAST / CCACT - 01.03.02
USE FOR ADVISORY COMMITTEE ON THE
APPLICATION OF SCIENCE AND TECHNOLOGY
TO DEVELOPMENT PRIOR TO JULY 1980 AND
THE ADVISORY COMMITTEE ON SCIENCE AND
TECHNOLOGY FOR DEVELOPMENT
THEREAFTER.
  TT: INTERNATIONAL ORGANIZATIONS
  BT: CSTD
  RT: SCIENCE
         TECHNOLOGY

ACCELERATED COURSES
COURS ACCELERES / CURSOS INTENSIVOS -
06.05.01
  UF: *INTENSIVE COURSES*
  TT: CURRICULUM
  BT: COURSES

ACCESS TO CULTURE
ACCES A LA CULTURE / ACCESO A LA
CULTURA - 05.02.03
  RT: CULTURE
         RIGHT TO EDUCATION

ACCESS TO EDUCATION
ACCES A L'EDUCATION / ACCESO A LA
EDUCACION - 06.02.02
  RT: EDUCATIONAL OPPORTUNITIES
         EDUCATIONAL SELECTION
         RIGHT TO EDUCATION

ACCESS TO INFORMATION
ACCES A L'INFORMATION / ACCESO A LA
INFORMACION - 19.01.01
  RT: DATA PROTECTION
         INFORMATION
         INFORMATION DISSEMINATION
         INFORMATION EXCHANGE
         INFORMATION SOURCES
         INFORMATION USERS

ACCESS TO MARKETS
ACCES AUX MARCHES / ACCESO A LOS
MERCADOS - 09.03.01
  UF: *MARKET ACCESS*
  RT: BOYCOTT
         EMBARGO
         MARKET
         TRADE AGREEMENTS

► ACCESS TO THE SEA
ACCES A LA MER / ACCESO AL MAR - 01.02.02
  RT: LANDLOCKED COUNTRIES
         RESOURCES EXPLOITATION

ACCESSIONS LISTS
LISTES D'ACQUISITIONS / CATALOGOS DE
ADQUISICIONES - 19.02.07
  TT: DOCUMENTS
  BT: SECONDARY DOCUMENTS
  RT: ACQUISITIONS

ACCIDENT INSURANCE
ASSURANCE CONTRE LES ACCIDENTS /
SEGURO CONTRA ACCIDENTES - 11.02.03
  TT: SERVICE INDUSTRY
  BT: INSURANCE
  RT: ACCIDENTS

ACCIDENT PREVENTION
  USE: SAFETY - 16.04.01

ACCIDENTS
ACCIDENTS / ACCIDENTES - 02.04.02
  NT: NUCLEAR ACCIDENTS
         OCCUPATIONAL ACCIDENTS
         TRAFFIC ACCIDENTS
  RT: ACCIDENT INSURANCE
         CAUSES OF DEATH
         DAMAGE
         SAFETY

ACCLIMATIZATION
ACCLIMATATION / ACLIMATACION - 17.02.01
  RT: CLIMATE

ACCOUNTANTS
COMPTABLES / CONTADORES - 13.09.09
  TT: HUMAN RESOURCES
         OCCUPATIONS
  BT: OFFICE WORKERS
  RT: ACCOUNTING

ACCOUNTING
COMPTABILITE / CONTABILIDAD - 12.09.00
  UF: *BOOKKEEPING*
  NT: COST ACCOUNTING
         NATIONAL ACCOUNTING
         PUBLIC ACCOUNTING
  RT: ACCOUNTANTS
         AUDITING

ACCT
ACCT / ACCT - 01.03.03
AGENCY FOR CULTURAL AND TECHNICAL
CO-OPERATION (AMONG FRENCH-SPEAKING
COUNTRIES).
  TT: INTERNATIONAL ORGANIZATIONS
  BT: INTERGOVERNMENTAL
         ORGANIZATIONS

ACCULTURATION
ACCULTURATION / ACULTURACION - 05.02.02
  RT: CULTURAL CHANGE
         CULTURAL IDENTITY
         CULTURAL RELATIONS
         CULTURE
         MIGRANT ASSIMILATION

ACCUMULATION RATE
TAUX D'ACCUMULATION / TASA DE
ACUMULACION - 03.01.02
  RT: CAPITAL FORMATION
         GROWTH RATE
         INVESTMENTS

ACDA
  USE: APDAC - 01.03.03

ACIDS
ACIDES / ACIDOS - 08.12.04
  NT: AMINO ACIDS
         INORGANIC ACIDS

ACOUSTIC POLLUTION
POLLUTION ACOUSTIQUE /
CONTAMINACION ACUSTICA - 16.03.04
  TT: POLLUTION
  BT: POLLUTION
  RT: NOISE
         NOISE CONTROL

ACOUSTICS
ACOUSTIQUE / ACUSTICA - 08.10.01
  TT: NATURAL SCIENCES

H3.3. Detailed faceted classification

This type of thesaurus arrangement involves the development of a faceted classification (see F4) as the systematic section, complemented by an alphabetical index or full alphabetical thesaurus. In this type of display the indexing terms are not mapped against a separate structure, but themselves form the faceted classification.

A faceted classification is the most suitable type of classification to use in a thesaurus because of its analytical/synthetic nature, which makes it compatible with thesaurus structure.

Existing classified thesauri and faceted classification systems, such as *BC2* (97), may be used as a source of arrangement and terminology.

Since the first faceted classified thesaurus, *Thesaurofacet*, there have been a number of versions differing from each other in the varying distribution of relational data between the systematic and alphabetical sections of the thesaurus.

H3.3.1. *Thesaurofacet*

In the *Thesaurofacet* (73) the division of information between the systematic and the alphabetical section was about equal, with the classification displaying the main hierarchies and related terms in a particular subject field, and the alphabetical section providing the information on related terms in other fields, polyhierarchies, scope notes and synonyms (Figure 16).

Example:

Systematic section		Alphabetical section	
H	**Mechanical components**	Fibre ropes HTN	
HT	Ropes	UF	Textile ropes
		BT(A)	Textile products
	(Components)	Ropes HT	
HTC	Strands	SN	Use for ropes generally
		NT(A)	Gymnastics ropes
	(Types – by material)	RT	Rescue equipment
HTN	Fibre ropes	Strands HTC	
HTR	Wire ropes	Wire ropes HTR	
		RT	Wires

H3.3.2. *Construction industry thesaurus* and 'Art and architecture thesaurus'

In the *Construction industry thesaurus* (86) (Figure 17) hierarchies and polyhierarchies are shown by indenting in the systematic display. Equivalent (non-preferred) terms are given after the preferred terms, preceded by the '=' sign. Associatively related terms, shown by indenting (see F3.3), do not occur in the display because the facets are homogeneous, due to the fundamental facet structure of the overall field of the thesaurus (see J7.1). The alphabetical display consists of an index to the systematic display, giving preferred and non-preferred terms without broader, narrower or related term details.

Figure 16. Detailed faceted classification
Thesaurofacet

Systematic display	Alphabetical display

Systematic display

Fuel technology   V

V	**FUEL TECHNOLOGY**
	* Power industries ZKT
➤ V2	**Fuels**
	* Nuclear fuels SE
	Subdivide by source:
V2B	Fossil fuels
	* Coal V3B
	* Fuel oils V5E
	* Gasoline V5C
	* Kerosene V5B
	* Natural gas V7A
	* Peat V3R
	* Petroleum V4D
	Subdivide by phase:
V2C	Solid fuels
	* Coal V3B
	* Peat V3R
	* Solid propellants V2T
	* Wood VJ2
V2D	Pulverised fuels
V2E	Liquid fuels
	* Fuel oils V5E
	* Gasoline V5C
	* Kerosene V5B
	* Liquid propellants V2M
	* Petroleum V4D
	* Natural gas liquids V5J
V2G	Gaseous fuels
	* Gaseous propellants V2L
	* Manufactured gas V7O
	* Natural gas V7A
	Subdivide by application:
V2H	Illuminating fuels
V2I	Aviation fuels
V2J	Jet fuels
V2K	Propellants
V2L	Gaseous propellants
V2M	Liquid propellants
V2N	Monopropellants
V2O	Bipropellants
V2P	Tripropellants
V2R	Hybrid propellants
V2T	Solid propellants
V2U	Homogenous solid
	propellants
V2V	Composite solid
	propellants
	For others, synthesise, for
	example:—
V2K/F7Q	Gelled propellants
V2K/UNN	Slurried propellants
V2X	Motor fuels
V2Y	Diesel fuels
V3	**COAL TECHNOLOGY**
	* Coal mining SUU
	* Coal mining industry ZKBA
	By products:
V3B	Coal
V3C	Anthracite

Alphabetical display

Fuel Rating (i.c. engines) *use*
Antiknock Rating

Fuel Rating (nuclear)		**EGB**
UF	Heat development in nuclear	
	reactors	
RT	Nuclear fuels	
BT(A)	Rating	

➤ **Fuels**		**V2**
RT	Antiknock ratings	
	Bunkers	
	Fuel consumption (i.c. engines)	
	Fuel distribution (i.c. engines)	
	Fuel systems	
	Heat processes (chemical	
	engineering)	
NT(A)	Nuclear fuels	
BT(A)	Materials by purpose	

Fuel Sprays		**OIM**
UF	Sprays (fuel)	
BT(A)	Sprays	

Fuel Systems		**OI**
RT	Bunkers	
	Fuel filters	
	Fuels	
BT(A)	Rocket engine components	

Fuel Tanks		**OIU**
RT	External stores	
BT(A)	Tanks	

Fuel Technology		**V**
RT	Power industries	

Fugacity		**COS**
RT	Vapour pressure	

Full   **AMN**

Full Employment   **ZJWHB**

Full Lift Single Seat Relief Valves		
		PNF/POC/PPL
Synth		
S	BT(A) Full lift valves	
S	Relief valves	
	Single seat valves	

Full Lift Valves		**POC**
NT(A)	Full lift single seat relief valves	

Full Pitch Windings   **KHQ**

Fulltime Work   **ZFEBB**

Full Wave Rectification *use*
Rectification

Full Wave Rectifiers *use*
Rectifiers

Fullway Valves *use*
Gate Valves

Fully Developed Flow   **CUD**

Fully Submerged Hydrofoil Craft   **RDJ**

Fumaric Acids   **HUFU(528)**

Functional Analysis		**BF8**
RT	Functionals	
	Function spaces	
BT(A)	Spaces (mathematics)	

Functional Block Diagrams *use*
Circuit Diagrams

Figure 17a. Detailed faceted classification
Construction industry thesaurus
Systematic display

Functional parts of construction works
Coverings

J21260	Minor coverings	
J21264	Decorative wall coverings	
J21266	Wall facings	
J21270	Wallpaper	
J21280	Wall tiles	
J21290	Trim	
J21295	Edgings	
J21300	Architraves	
J21310	Skirting	
J21330	Dadoes	
J21350	Pelmets	
J21360	Roses	
J21370	Bosses	
J21380	Cover beads	
J21390	Cover strips	
J21400	Protective coverings for services	
J21410	Casing = Cases	
J21420	Casing (Electrical) *J34544	
J21430	Socks	
J21440	Cable socks	
J21450	Jackets	
J21460	➤ Insulating jackets	
J21470	Steam jackets	
J21480	Coverings for openings	
J21490	Cover plates = Covers	
J21500	Trench covers	
J21510	Manhole covers	
J21520	Access covers	
J21530	Lids	
J23010	Barriers = Stops	
J23030	Gratings = Anti foul grids = Grids	*Barriers by form*
J23050	Cavities *J01330	
J23054	Bulkheads	
J23056	Buffers = Bumpers	
J23060	Screens	
J23065	Curtains	
J23068	Flyscreens	
J23070	Guards = Fences = Fencing	*Barriers by what barred*
J23072	Strained wire fences	
J23074	Railings = Unclimable fences = Vertical bar fences	
J23076	Chain link fences	
J23078	Post and panel fences	
J23080	Continuous bar fences	
J23082	Pale fences	
J23084	Pales	*Parts of fences*
J23086	Tree guards	
J23090	Fluid, sound, etc. barriers	
J23095	Baffles	
J23100	Fire barriers	
J23110	Heat and light barriers	
J23112	Shades = Shading	
J23114	Sun shades = Sun breakers	
J23116	Louvres	
J23120	Blinds *J23690	
J23130	Shutters *J23680	
J23200	Insulation	*Prevent passage of heat, electricity, sound*
J23210	Thermal insulation	
J23220	Loose fill insulants	
J23230	Pipe insulation	
J23240	➤ Insulating jackets *J21460	

Figure 17b. Detailed faceted classification
Construction industry thesaurus
Alphabetical display

Insulating (Operations)	G06730	Interceptors		
		USE Intercepting traps	J51682	
Insulating (Properties)	E15600	Interchangeable	E02000	
Insulating board	J07750	Interchanges	K25150	
Insulating jackets	J21460 (J23240)	UF Grade separated junctions		
		Intercom systems	J69806	
Insulating materials	H53850	Intercoolers	J55352	
Insulation	J23200	UF Desuperheaters		
Insulation properties	E15590	Interdependence	B25520	
Insurance	B39030	Interest rates	B38660	
Insurance premiums		Interference (Optical effects)	B02840	
USE Premiums	B39040	Interference (Properties)	E00740	
Integral	E07060	Interference (Telecommunications)	B03840	
UF Integrated				
Integrated		Interference by the state		
USE Integral	E07060	USE State intervention	B29410	
Integrated circuits	J34634	Interferometry	B06137	
Integrated design	G05030	Interim certificates	F15830	
Integrating meters	J38330	Interim payments		
Integration	B00280	USE Progress payments	B38150	
Intensifying		Interior		
USE Increasing	G08270	USE Internal	E07850	
Intensity (Density)	E02220	Interior design	G04990	
Intensity (Flux)	E25390 (E56050)	Interior designers	F07640	
UF Flux density		Interior lighting	J69706	
Light density		Interior parts	K02390	
Intensity level	E25510 (E56290)	Interior properties	E45680	
Intensive care units	K30600	Interiors	J00330	
		UF Insides		
Intensive farming	B39830	Interlacing	G34770	
Intensive rearing spaces	K12950	Interlock	B00715	
Inter		Interlocked grain	H40750	
USE Between	E07970	UF Interlocking grain		
Inter polymers		Interlocking	G34820	
USE Copolymers	H33110	Interlocking grain		
Interacting	G80100	USE Interlocked grain	H40750	
Interaction properties	E14600	Interlocking joints	J15120	
Intercepting traps	J51682	UF Side locking joints		
UF Disconnecting traps				
Interceptors		Interlocking panels	J06811	

In the more recent 'Art and architecture thesaurus' (76), the systematic display shows by indenting hierarchical, polyhierarchical and also whole–part relationships (Figure 19). Equivalent terms are given after the preferred terms, separated by an oblique sign. Both preferred and non-preferred terms are followed by source codes. The first column on the left contains the hierarchy line numbers within the BW (Built Works) hierarchy, and the second column indicates the level of indentation. The alphabetical display, as in the *Construction industry thesaurus*, is no more than an index to the systematic display, giving preferred and non-preferred terms, with their source codes, but as yet no hierarchical or associative relationships.

H3.3.3. BSI *ROOT thesaurus* style

In other faceted thesauri a style has developed in which all the elements and relationships are given in the systematic display, so that a full alphabetical thesaurus may be derived from it automatically, if required. The *UNESCO thesaurus* (71) was an interim stage in this development, which was finalized in the BSI *ROOT thesaurus* (81) format.

The BSI *ROOT thesaurus* (Figure 18), and thesauri using the *ROOT* format, such as the *Thesaurus on youth* (74) and the *ECOT thesaurus* (70), place all definitional and relational data in the systematic section, i.e., scope notes (SN), equivalence relations (UF) and main broader, narrower and related terms shown by indenting. Additional related terms are indicated by *RT and polyhierarchies are indicated by *BT/*NT. References to polyhierarchical and related terms in other parts of the display are accompanied by the notation showing where the term is located.

Example:

BSI ROOT thesaurus style systematic display

H	**Mechanical components**	
HT	Ropes	
	SN Use for Ropes generally	
	*NT Gymnastics ropes	XVG.N
	*RT Rescue equipment	SNK
	(Components)	
HTC *(RT)*	Strands	
	(Types – by material)	
HTN	Fibre ropes	
	UF Textile ropes	
	*BT Textile products	UMN
HTR	Wire ropes	
	*RT Wires	PVL

Figure 18. Detailed faceted classification
ROOT thesaurus

Systematic display

K	**Electrotechnology**

KB/KO	**Electrical engineering** (continued)
KE/KJ	**Electrical equipment** (continued)
KIP	**Electrical protection equipment** (continued)
KIP.V	Electric contact protection
	* —Electric contacts KNR

(By construction)

KIP.W	Double electrical insulation
	* —Electrical insulation CYB.K
	* —Electrical insulation devices KNX

(By connection to earth)

KIP.X	Earthing
	=Earth (electric)
	=Earthing systems
	=Electric grounding
	=Grounding (electric)
	* —Earthing reactors KHC.E
KIP.XE	Earth electrodes
	* —Electrodes KNW
KIP.XH	Earth conductors
	=Protective conductors
	* <Electric conductors KNN
KIP.XN	Earthing switches
	=Automatic earthing switches
	* <Switches KJH
KIP.XR	Neutral conductors
	* <Electric conductors KNN

KJ	**Switchgear**
	* >Fuses KIP.M
	* —Bus-bars KNN.B
	* —Electric control equipment KIB
	* —Switching substations KDS.SH
KJC ➡	Circuit-breakers
	=Air-break circuit-breakers
	=Air circuit-breakers
	* >Earth-leakage circuit-breakers KIP.Q
	* >Relay circuit-breakers KIP.PC
	* —Operating time MBC.DP
	* —Switch-fuses KJH.C
	* —Switches KJH

(By size)

KJC.C	Miniature circuit-breakers
	* —Fuses KIP.M

(By operating medium)

KJC.E	Oil circuit-breakers
KJC.G	Gas-blast circuit-breakers
KJC.GC	Air-blast circuit-breakers
KJC.H	Vacuum circuit-breakers
	* <Vacuum devices NPT

(By design)

KJC.M	Tri-pole circuit-breakers
	=Triple-pole circuit-breakers

Alphabetical display

Cinematography   LPM
- <   Photography
- −   Sprockets (cinematography)
- * −   Film-making   ZWW.CW
- * −   Film studios   RDH.X
- * −   Location lighting   RLH.T
- * −   Motion-picture cameras   LQB.C
- * −   Motion-picture projectors   LQD.C
- * −   Recording engineering   LN
- * −   Special effects (photography)   LPO

Cineole   DVG.P
- −   Terpene hydrocarbons

Cinnamon   IIG.I
- <   Spices

Cinnamon   IIG.I
- +   Essential oils   VMF/VMH
- = * *   Oil of cinnamon   VMG.D

Circles (geometry)   CCG.J
- −   Arcs of a circle
- −   Geometry

Circling guidance lights
- →   Aeronautical ground lights   RLH.S

Circlips   NWU.FF
- <   Spring retaining rings

Circuit analysis
- →   Network analysis (circuits)   KPE

Circuit-breaker components   KJC.R
- >   Arc control devices
- >   Interrupters (circuit-breakers)
- >   Tripping mechanisms (circuit-breakers)
- −   Circuit-breakers

➡   **Circuit-breakers**   KJC
- =   Air-break circuit-breakers
- =   Air circuit-breakers
- <   Switchgear
- >   Gas-blast circuit-breakers
- >   Miniature circuit-breakers
- >   Oil circuit-breakers
- >   Overcurrent circuit-breakers
- >   Tri-pole circuit-breakers
- >   Vacuum circuit-breakers
- −   Breaking capacity
- −   Circuit-breaker components
- −   Making capacity
- −   Recovery voltage
- * >   Earth-leakage circuit-breakers   KIP.Q
- * >   Relay circuit-breakers   KIP.PC
- * −   Operating time   MBC.DP
- * −   Switch-fuses   KJH.C
- * −   Switches   KJH

Circuit design
- →   Network synthesis   KPG

Figure 19a. Detailed faceted classification
'Art and architecture thesaurus'
Hierarchical display
(Symbols and letters following terms are source codes)

```
 1   0   Single built works *S        Single Built Works: partial listing
 2   1   <single built works by specific type>
 3   2   <single built works by function>
 4   3
 5   4   Dwellings *L /Domestic architecture *R $L /Domestic facilities *S /Habitations *S /Residences @L
 6           /Residential architecture *S
 7           /Residential buildings *S
 8           /Residential facilities *S
 9   5   Houses *AB /Homes *S
10   6   <houses by form>
11   7   <houses by form: plan>
12   8   Attached houses *S
13   9   Row houses *LRA /Row dwellings *S /Group houses *S /Town houses *S /Townhouses *S
14  10   Brownstones *S. /Brownstone houses *S
15  10   Terraced houses @B /Terrace houses *LR $B /Terraces *S
16   8   Detached houses *S /Detached domestic architecture *S /Detached dwellings *S
17   8   Double-pen houses *S /Double-fronted houses *S /Hall-and-parlor houses *S
18   9   Dogtrots *S /Dogtrot houses *S
19   9   I-houses *S
20   9   Saddlebag houses *S
21   8   Double-pile houses *S
22   8   Longhouses *S
23   8   Octagonal houses @A /Octagons *S
24   8   Oval houses $B
25   8   Round houses @A /Roundhouses *S
26   8   Semi-detached houses *S /Semi-detached dwellings *S
27   8   Shotgun houses *S
28   8   Single-pen houses *S /Half houses *S /Single-fronted houses *S
29   8   Single-pile houses *S
30   7   <houses by form: roof orientation>
31   8   Gable front houses *S /Front gabled houses *S
32   8   Gable-front-and-wing houses *S
33   8   Side gabled houses *S
34   6   <houses by function>
35   7   Seasonal dwellings *S
36   8   Second homes *L
37   8   Summer houses *S /Summer homes *L /Summerhouses *S
38   9   Summer cottages *S
39   8   Vacation houses *A /Holiday houses @B /Weekend houses @B
40   9   Overnight cabins *S
41   9   Vacation cabins *S
42   7   Sunday houses *S
```

Figure 19b. Detailed faceted classification
'Art and architecture thesaurus'
Alphabetical display
(Symbols and letters following terms are source codes)

```
BW 46  8 Architect-designed houses *L $AB
BW 12  8 Attached houses *S
BW 44  7 Bastel houses *S
         Bastille houses *S...................BW 44  7 Bastel houses *S
         Bastle houses *A @B..................BW 44  7 Bastel houses *S
BW 71  8 Beach houses *A @R
BW 59 10 Borgen @R
         Brownstone houses *S.................BW 14 10 Brownstones *S
BW 14 10 Brownstones *S
BW 47  ? Builder-designed houses $B
BW 6? 10 Casinos *S
BW 64 10 Colonica *S.........................BW 64 10 Colonicae *S
BW 64 10 Colonicae *S
BW 58  9 Country homes *L @A.................BW 58  9 Country houses *A @B
BW 58  9 Country houses *A @B................BW 58  9 Country houses *A @B
BW 45  7 Country seats *S....................
         Custom-designed houses *S
         Dacha $S............................BW 61 10 Dachas *S
BW 61 10 Dachas *S
         Datcha $S...........................BW 61 10 Dachas *S
         Demonstration houses @B.............BW 49  7 Model houses *L @B
         Detached domestic architecture *S...BW 16  8 Detached houses *S
         Detached dwellings *S...............BW 16  8 Detached houses *S
BW 16  8 Detached houses *S
         Dogtrot houses *S...................BW 18  9 Dogtrots *S
BW 18  9 Dogtrots *S
         Domestic architecture *R $L.........BW  5  4 Dwellings *L
         Domestic facilities *S..............BW  5  4 Dwellings *L
         Double-fronted houses *S............BW 17  8 Double-pen houses *S
BW 17  8 Double-pen houses *S
BW 21  8 Double-pile houses *S
BW  5  4 Dwellings *L
         Earth covered houses @L.............BW 72  8 Earth sheltered houses *LA
BW 80  7 Earth lodges *S
BW 72  8 Earth sheltered houses *LA
         Entrance lodges *S..................BW 75  8 Gatehouses *RB
         Estates $R..........................BW 58  9 Country houses *A @B
         Farm houses @LA.....................BW 63  9 Farmhouses *LA
BW 63  9 Farmhouses *LA
         Front gabled houses *S..............BW 31  8 Gable front houses *S
BW 31  8 Gable front houses *S
BW 32  8 Gable-front-and-wing houses *S
```

The amount of information in the alphabetical section may vary. As the systematic section gives all relational information an alphabetical index may suffice, as in the *Thesaurus on youth* (see Figure 20) where the index contains only preferred and non-preferred index terms. On the other hand, an alphabetical thesaurus is a useful format for online handling and merging with other thesauri. A full alphabetical section repeats the scope notes, equivalence relationships, hierarchies, and related terms, shown by indenting in the display, and the polyhierarchies and related terms, shown as cross-references. The broader and narrower terms are limited to the hierarchical level above and below the preferred term. The indented terms in the display which are associatively related and not narrower terms to their superordinate terms – for example, Strands in the above example (page 92) – should be coded (RT) before the alphabetical display is generated.

Example:

BSI ROOT thesaurus style alphabetical display

Fibre ropes   HTN
   UF   Textile ropes
   BT   Ropes
   *BT   Textile products   UMN
Ropes   HT
   SN   Use for Ropes generally
   BT   Mechanical components
   NT   Fibre ropes
        Wire ropes
   RT   Strands
   *NT   Gymnastics ropes   XVG.N
   *RT   Rescue equipment   SNK
Strands   HTC
   RT   Ropes
Wire ropes   HTR
   BT   Ropes
   *RT   Wires   PVL

The asterisked terms (*BT/*NT/*RT) may be interfiled if preferred with the BT/NT/RT sequence derived from the indented entries in the display, although it would be useful to retain the notation following the asterisked term, as this gives direct access to the appropriate part of the systematic display where the term is located. (N.B. This is different from the notation for the preferred terms under which they are listed.)

Example:

Ropes   HT
   SN   Use for Ropes generally
   BT   Mechanical components
   NT   Fibre ropes
        Gymnastics ropes   XVG.N
        Wire ropes
   RT   Rescue equipment   SNK
        Strands

This ROOT style of thesaurus is helpful for the compiler as all the intellectual effort takes place at the stage of creating the systematic section. The alphabetical section may be derived by clerical effort or computer program from the systematic section (25).

H3.3.4. Polyhierarchies in systematic displays

ISO 2788 and BS 5723 show a layout of a systematic section in which indexing terms with more than one broader term are placed in each appropriate hierarchy. The *Construction industry thesaurus* (see Figure 17) deals with polyhierarchies in this way.

Example:

Systematic display

H		**Mechanical components**
		…
HT		Ropes
		(Components)
HTC	*(RT)*	Strands
		(Types – by material)
→ HTN		Fibre ropes
		UF Textile ropes
HTR		Wire ropes
		*RT Wires PVL
		(Types – by application)
→ HTW		Gymnastic ropes
		UF Climbing ropes
…		…
UM		**Textile technology**
		…
UMN	*(RT)*	Textile products
UMN.C		Yarn
UMN.K		Cloth
→ UMN.T		Fibre ropes
		UF Textile ropes
…		…
XV		**Leisure equipment**
XVG		Gymnastic equipment
XVG.C		Springboards
UVG.E		Wall bars
UVG.G		Vaulting bars
→ UNG.N		Gymnastic ropes
		UF Climbing ropes

Figure 20a. Detailed faceted classification
Thesaurus on youth
Systematic display

YOUTH AND COMMUNITY SERVICE

QQ	**YOUTH AND COMMUNITY SERVICE PROVISION** (cont.)
QS	**YOUTH AND COMMUNITY SERVICE ACTIVITIES** (cont.)
QT	**Youth clubs** (cont.)
QU	Youth club members (cont.)

QUG   Senior youth club members

QUH   Young adult youth club members
       * BT Young adults   JHM

➤ QV   Youth club programmes
       UF Youth club activities
       * BT Programmes   GEL
       * RT Youth service based community service   RP

       [Note

       (By administration)

       Combine with terms under Administrative science G, e.g.
       Youth club programmes : Programming QV:GEK]

QW   Youth club programmes - by specific activities ●

       [Note
       Combine with terms under Education B, Communities
       and community work P, Leisure V, and Arts W, e.g.
       Youth club programmes : Educational courses QW:BI
       Youth club programmes : Community radio QW:PPL
       Youth club programmes : Sport QW:VH
       Youth club programmes : Indoor games QW:VQ
       Youth club programmes : Holidays QW:VS
       Youth club programmes : Handicrafts QW:WG]

       (By types)

QX   Youth club types

       (By type of location)

       [Note. Combine with terms under Human settlement KC,
       e.g.]

QX:KE   ***Rural youth clubs*
       USE Youth club types   QX
       + Rural areas   KE

       (By religion, race, sex, etc.)

QXC   Church youth clubs
       * BT Church youth provision   QQP
       * RT Church work   UUH
       Church youth organisations   QHD
       Church youth workers   QOW

Figure 20b. Detailed faceted classification
Thesaurus on youth
Index

Young Womens Christian Association QKT
　UF　YWCA
Young workers HHB
　UF　Young wage earners
Young workers associations HBR
　UF　Youth forums in industry
Youngest child JPJ
Youth (adolescence)
　use　Adolescence
Youth action workers
　use　Young volunteer organisers
Youth advisory services
　use　Counselling services
Youth affairs A
　SN　This section is for items on youth matters
　　　at a general level. Items on Youth and
　　　community service are not to be indexed
　　　here but at schedule Q
Youth Affairs Lobby AJB
Youth and Community Bill EED
Youth and community education officers
QOC
Youth and community personnel QO
　UF　Leaders (youth)
　　　Youth leaders
　　　Youth service personnel
Youth and community service Q
　UF　Youth service
Youth and community service activities QS
Youth and community service agencies QB
Youth and community service interagency
relations QBL
Youth and community service-I.T. relations
NFM
Youth and community service-police relations
　use　Police-youth service relations
Youth and community service projects QZ
　UF　Youth service projects
Youth and community service provision QQ
　UF　Youth service provision
Youth and community service-social services
relations QBP
　UF　Social services-youth service relations
Youth and community work
　use　Youth work
Youth and community worker professional
associations QN
Youth Camping Association of Great Britain
QKV
Youth centre wardens QOT
Youth centres QY
Youth charter EXF
Youth club activities
　use　Youth club programmes
Youth club leaders
.　use　Youth club workers
Youth club members QU
　UF　Members (youth club)
➤ **Youth club programmes** QV/QW
　UF　Youth club activities
Youth club types QX
Youth club workers QOV
　UF　Youth club leaders
Youth clubs QT
Youth councils AKC
Youth counselling services
　use　Counselling services
Youth counsellors
　use　Counsellors
Youth counter-cultures TNM
Youth cultures TM
　UF　Adolescent cultures

　　Youth subcultures
Youth employment HH
Youth forums in industry
　use　Young workers associations
Youth groups JRK
Youth hostels VVN
　UF　Hostelling
Youth Hostels Association QKW
Youth leaders
　use　Youth and community personnel
Youth Opportunities Programme HJ
　UF　YOP
Youth Opportunities Programme personnel
HJC
Youth Opportunities Programme recipients
HJD
　UF　Recipients (Youth Opportunities Programme)
Youth orchestras WMP
Youth organisations AD
Youth policy AB
Youth problems AAP
　SN　For general surveys only. Prefer terms for
　　　specific problem where possible
　UF　Problems (youth)
Youth service
　use　Youth and community service
Youth service based community service RP
　SN　For general surveys of activities and
　　　services
Youth Service Development Council QDX
Youth Service Forum QDF
Youth service personnel
　use　Youth and community personnel
Youth service projects
　use　Youth and community service projects
Youth service provision
　use　Youth and community service provision
Youth social services
　use　Youth social work
Youth social work MO
　UF　Youth social services
Youth social workers MHQ
Youth subcultures
　use　Youth cultures
Youth tutors QOQ
　UF　Teacher leaders
　　　Tutor wardens
　　　Tutors (youth)
Youth unemployment HI
Youth unemployment programmes HIW
Youth wings QQE
Youth work QP
　UF　Youth and community work
Youth work training officers QOR
Youthaid MEU
Yugoslavia 6LF
YWCA
　use　Young Womens Christian Association

　　　Z

Zaire 6VLK
Zambia 6VRH
Zen Buddhism UPU
Zimbabwe 6VRJ
　UF　Rhodesia
Zoological gardens KTG
　UF　Zoos
Zoology YDE
　UF　Animal biology
Zoos
　use　Zoological gardens

Example of polyhierarchies in systematic displays (cont.)

  Alphabetical display

Fibre ropes   HTN; UMN.T
    UF Textile ropes
    BT Ropes
        Textile products
Gymnastic ropes   HTW; XVG.N
    UF Climbing ropes
    BT Gymnastics equipment
        Ropes
Ropes   HT
    SN Use for Ropes generally
    BT Mechanical components
    NT Fibre ropes
        Gymnastic ropes
        Wire ropes
    RT Strands
Strands   HTC
    RT Ropes
Wire ropes   HTR
    BT Ropes
    RT Wires   PVL

This method differs from the BSI ROOT system approach which places an indexing term in one preferred hierarchy and makes reference from it to broader terms in other hierarchies using the code *BT followed by the appropriate class number. Under these broader terms reciprocal *NT references are made to the indexing term. (See H3.3.3, J7.2.1 (page 132) and Figure 35.)

The multiple placing of indexing terms gives the most detailed analysis of each subject field, as in each location the indexing term has to be carefully placed in the correct facets and arrays. There is then no bias in favour of analysing one subject field more fully than another. Another advantage is that a term may be retrieved in a truncated search on notation for all its broader terms. For example, searching on HT* Ropes or UMN* Textile products will retrieve Fibre ropes, whereas in the preferred term layout a search on UMN* would not retrieve the term as it lacks a class mark in this subject field. On the other hand, when there is frequent repetition of lengthy hierarchies, it requires more work for the compiler and also overloads the display.

H4. Graphic display

Indexing terms and their interrelationships may be displayed in the form of a two-dimensional figure from which the user may select those terms that are appropriate. Graphic displays help to improve access and may also be a useful tool during thesaurus construction in bringing related concepts together in semantic clusters.

Where there are detailed hierarchies and numerous associative relationships to display, a large number of charts will be necessary to portray relationships without overcrowding on individual charts. (This could result in an unwieldy number of displays which are difficult to handle and expensive to print.)

There are three main types of graphic display: family tree structures, arrowgraphs, and terminographs or box charts.

H4.1 Family tree structures

In this layout the broadest term occurs at the head of the display and narrower terms are printed in subordinate positions, the relationship being indicated by vertical connecting lines. Scope notes, equivalence relationships, polyhierarchies, and related terms are usually shown only in the accompanying alphabetical section. Each family tree diagram is given a notation, which is quoted as the address of all the terms in the diagram.

Example:

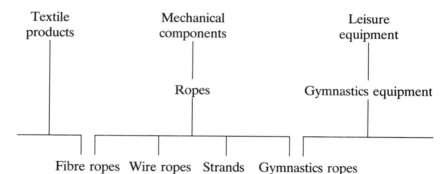

See also Figure 21, an extract from the Institute for the Study of Drug Dependence's *ISDD thesaurus* (87). The family tree structures in this thesaurus are the graphic equivalent of separate machine-derived hierarchies, as found in the *INSPEC thesaurus*, and others (see H2.1). The tree structures are located via the TT (top term) code in the alphabetical display. Unlike the *INSPEC thesaurus* hierarchies, these tree structures were the source of, and not derived from, the hierarchical relationships in the alphabetical display. Another thesaurus containing tree structures is the *Thesaurus of terms in copper technology* (79).

Family tree structures may lack equivalence relationships and do not usually differentiate between broader and narrower and related terms in the diagram itself. However, these relationships are shown in the *PRECIS* thesaurus networks (Figure 22). Vertical lines and the code $o show general BT/NT relationships, horizontal lines and code $m equivalence relationships, and inclined lines and code $n associative relationships.

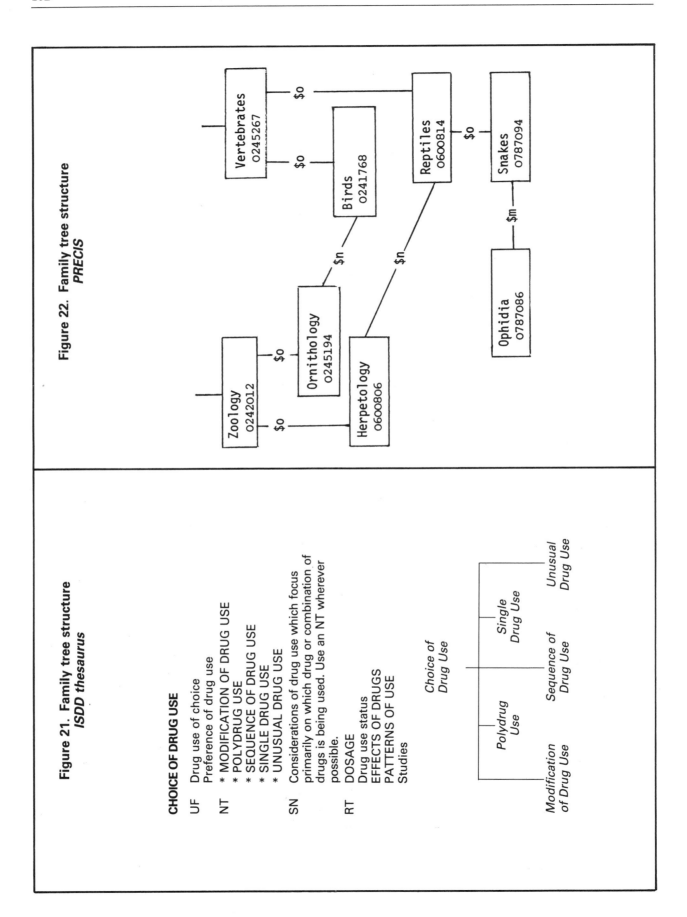

Figure 22. Family tree structure
PRECIS

Vertebrates
0245267

$o

$o

Birds
0241768

Reptiles
06o0814

$o

Snakes
0787094

$n

$n

$m

Ornithology
0245194

Herpetology
06o0806

Ophidia
0787086

Zoology
0242012

$o

$o

Figure 21. Family tree structure
ISDD thesaurus

CHOICE OF DRUG USE

UF   Drug use of choice
      Preference of drug use

NT   * MODIFICATION OF DRUG USE
      * POLYDRUG USE
      * SEQUENCE OF DRUG USE
      * SINGLE DRUG USE
      * UNUSUAL DRUG USE

SN   Considerations of drug use which focus
      primarily on which drug or combination of
      drugs is being used. Use an NT wherever
      possible.

RT   DOSAGE
      Drug use status
      EFFECTS OF DRUGS
      PATTERNS OF USE
      Studies

*Choice of
Drug Use*

*Polydrug
Use*

*Single
Drug Use*

*Unusual
Drug Use*

*Modification
of Drug Use*

*Sequence of
Drug Use*

H4.2 Arrowgraphs

Arrowgraphs are displays in the form of charts representing a number of specific subject fields and subfields. The chart may be marked with grids. Each chart has its own distinguishing notation, and the terms displayed in the chart may be located by the reference to the chart notation and to the specific grid reference number if a grid is used.

The broadest term is placed towards the centre of the chart in bold type (see Figure 23a). Narrower (and related) terms are printed in other positions within the grid, and hierarchical levels are shown by connecting arrows or lines pointing from the higher to the lower generic level; associatively related terms may be shown by connected two-way arrow systems or by broken lines. Reference is made to related indexing terms outside the groups represented in the chart, giving the relevant notation in the appropriate chart. Equivalence relations and scope notes are not usually shown on arrowgraphs. The alphabetical section may consist of no more than an index to the chart numbers of the indexing terms, but the data in the alphabetical section could include scope notes, equivalence relations, broader, narrower and related terms, as in Figure 23b. This form of layout is decribed fully in a paper by Rolling (59).

The earliest diagram with arrows showing term relationships was the *TDCK circular thesaurus system* of 1963 (100) published by the Netherlands Armed Forces Technical Documentation and Information Centre. In 1966–67 Rolling compiled the *EURATOM thesaurus* (88) for the Commission of the European Communities, which featured arrowgraphs, and later he developed the trilingual SDIM thesaurus of 1974 (96) in the field of metallurgy. Arrowgraphs are also found in the multilingual *International Road Research Documentation (IRRD) thesaurus* (92) which includes about fifty arrowgraphs complemented by an alphabetical section (see Figure 24).

H4.3. Terminographs/box charts

Another type of graphic display is the terminograph or box chart found in Volume 3 of *SPINES thesaurus* (99) and in the 1984 edition of the *EUDISED thesaurus* (109). In the *EUDISED thesaurus* (see Figure 25), there are 42 subfields or microthesauri, each represented by a terminograph, set out on a single page, which is identified in the bottom right-hand corner by a two-digit serial number followed by the title of the microthesaurus. Each terminograph contains an inner frame enclosing all the preferred terms in the microthesaurus. These preferred terms are listed hierarchically under the top terms (underlined) inside boxes. The steps of the hierarchy within the boxes are shown by the indenting of subordinate terms. Associative relationships between the preferred terms in the same microthesaurus are shown by thick lines for relations between top terms, medium lines for relations between a top term and another preferred term, and thin lines between preferred terms that are not top terms. Outside the frame appear preferred terms referring to other microthesauri but linked to the preferred terms within the microthesaurus by some associative relationship (indicated by a line without an arrow) or by a polyhierarchical relation (shown as a double arrowed line). On the left of each external preferred term appears the number(s) of the microthesaurus to which it belongs. Non-preferred terms are not shown in the terminograph. The link between the terms in

Figure 23a. Graphic display – arrowgraph

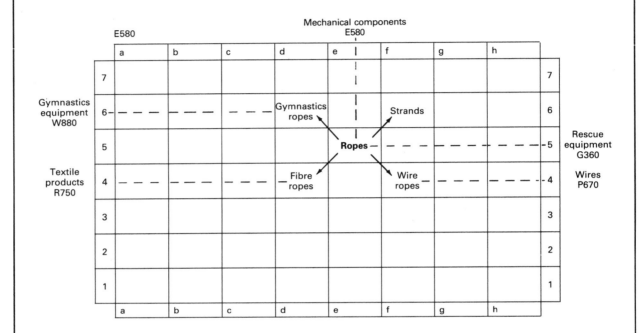

Figure 23b. Alphabetical index to arrowgraph

Fibre ropes   E580.d4
   BT   Ropes
           Textile products

Gymnastics equipment   W880.d4
   NT   Gymnastics ropes

Gymnastics ropes   E580.d6
   BT   Gymnastics equipment
           Ropes

Mechanical components   E500.e5
   NT   Ropes

Rescue equipment   G360.c3
   RT   Ropes

Ropes   E580.e5
   BT   Mechanical components

Ropes (cont.)
   NT   Fibre ropes
           Gymnastics ropes
           Wire ropes
   RT   Rescue equipment
           Strands

Strands   E580.f6
   RT   Ropes

Textile products   R750.f3
   NT   Fibre ropes

Wire ropes   E580.f4
   BT   Ropes
   RT   Wires

Wires   P670.d5
   RT   Wire ropes

105

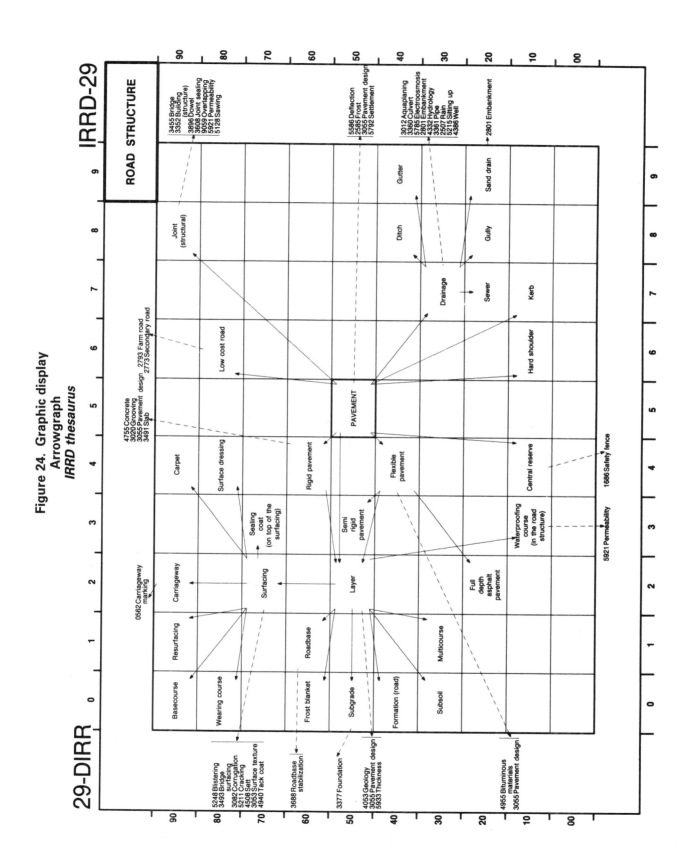

Figure 24. Graphic display Arrowgraph *IRRD thesaurus*

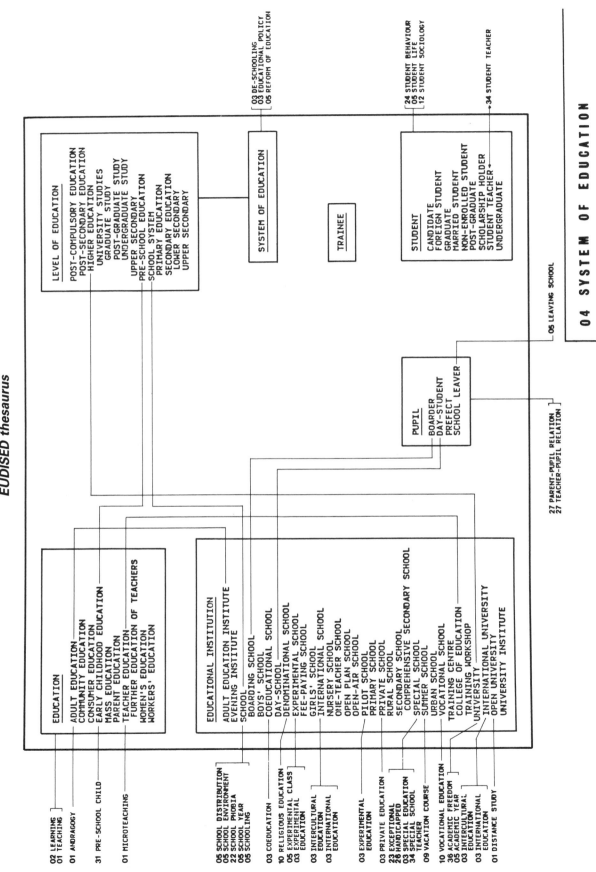

Figure 25. Graphic display
Terminograph
EUDISED thesaurus

the alphabetical listing and in the terminograph is the terminograph number. All terms in the one microthesaurus have the same number but are not precisely located on the page by a specific grid reference number, as in the arrowgraph.

More detailed accounts of the history and development of graphic displays may be found in Gilchrist (36, pp. 35–38, 89–92) and Foskett (32).

Section I Special types of thesauri

I1. Multilingual thesauri

The problems of multilingual thesaurus construction are no worse, in kind, than those of monolingual thesaurus construction; providing, of course, that there are competent linguists available. Perhaps the most difficult aspect is that of human organization, often involving the work of international committees.

The relevant standard here is ISO 5964: 1985: *Guidelines for the establishment and development of multilingual thesauri* (43), the equivalent to British Standard 6723: 1985 (15), which states clearly right at the start: 'The guidelines given in this International Standard should be used in conjunction with ISO 2788, and regarded as an extension of the scope of the monolingual guidelines. It is considered that the majority of procedures and recommendations contained in ISO 2788 are equally valid for a multilingual thesaurus'. This can be seen to be sound advice when it is considered that the majority of descriptors are nouns (see D3.1) and, more importantly, that thesaurus compilation is concerned with the identification of the concepts behind the words.

Thus, the handling of descriptors in multilingual thesauri is much the same as in monolingual work, with the added variety of morphologies arising from the different language forms. It may be useful, then, to know that languages are classified broadly into four forms:

○ Inflectional languages, such as Latin, which use case-endings. These root-suffixes qualify the nouns and verbs.

○ Agglutinative languages, such as Turkish, Finnish and Hungarian where the root-suffixes can, and regularly do, stand as separate words.

○ Isolating languages, such as Chinese, which make no use of inflection, agglutination or prepositions.

○ Analytical languages, such as English, which use word order, auxiliary words and some vestiges of inflection to provide the grammatical structure.

However, though the above knowledge may be useful, it is not so important as a good working knowledge of the languages being handled, including the socio-cultural nuances, particularly present in non-scientific subjects.

I1.1 Source and target thesauri
The first decision to be made in the multilingual situation is which is to be the 'source language'; and this should obtain whether the work is to be started *ab initio* or existing schemes are to be reconciled and merged.

The source language is defined as 'that language which serves as a starting point when a preferred term is translated into its nearest equivalent term or terms in a second language'. This second language and any subsequent languages are known as 'target languages'. No implication of status should be made in the use of the terms 'source' and 'targets', and the choice of the source language should be made on pragmatic grounds, no one language having dominance over any other. Thus, in the compilation work, it will be important to feed back concepts and translations continuously from each target language, taken in turn, to the source language.

I1.2. Equivalences

BS 6723 contains a table, reproduced in Figure 26, showing five degrees of equivalence, and these are discussed, in turn, below.

○ Exact equivalence

This is the analogue of the true synonym and is dealt with straightforwardly, as in the following example.

English	French	German
PHYSICS	= PHYSIQUE	= PHYSIK

○ Inexact equivalence

This is the analogue of the near synonym and, again, is dealt with as in monolingual thesauri, i.e., the near synonyms are regarded, for indexing purposes, as being equivalent, as in the following example.

German	French	English
GEDECK	= MENU	= MENUS

where the English equivalent is a 'loan term' from the French, and normally expressed in the plural, whereas the German and French standards prefer the singular form for descriptors.

○ Partial equivalence

This is similar to the case of the near synonym but in which one of the terms strictly viewed denotes a slightly broader or narrower concept. Thus, the two terms can either be treated as synonyms, or one can be recognized as being broader, and dealt with accordingly. The example given in ISO 5964 is the well-known case of the German word *'Wissenschaft'* which has a broader connotation than the English word 'science'.

○ Single-to-multiple equivalence

This is the most complex situation and the one which requires the most thoughtful analysis. Essentially, there are three separate, though similar, situations, each having at least three solutions.

Situation 1: ˌ where a term does not exist in another language but two or more narrower terms do, which in combination cover the broader concept.

Situation 2: similar to situation 1, but where factoring (see E2.4.2) can be employed.

Situation 3: where two generic terms exist in one language and only one in another, it not being clear which of the two generic terms is the most appropriate.

Figure 26. Degrees of equivalence

Case	Source language	Target language
1 — Exact equivalence		
2 — Inexact equivalence		
3 — Partial equivalence		
4 — Single-to-multiple equivalence		
5 — Non-equivalence		

acceptable term exists

acceptable term does not exist

The solutions differ in the degree of detail which can be incorporated and in the accuracy with which the concepts in the two languages are equated. One trick which is to be found throughout these examples is the use of the 'loan term'. For example, in the case of the German word *'Wissenschaft'*, this could be included in the English thesaurus clearly marked as a loan term from the German and shown as being a BT to science. Whereas this seems not only permissible but useful where a particular word has a local and socio-cultural content, it is be be avoided in those cases where the underlying concepts can be equated, as can be seen in the examples which follow.

Example of situation 1

The English word 'skidding' has no equivalent in German but there exist the two words, *Rutschen*, which means 'forward skidding', and *Schleudern* which means 'sideways skidding'. Apart from the deprecated denoting of the English word 'skidding' as a loan term to the German (or presumably both *Rutschen* and *Schleudern* to the English) there are two courses of action:

(a) to recognize skidding as the addition of *Rutschen* and *Schleudern*

(b) to regard *Rutschen* and *Schleudern* as variations of an English homograph 'skidding'.

In practice the combination of (a) and (b) is the preferred solution, achieving all the equivalents, as shown below:

SKIDDING   = RUTSCHEN + SCHLEUDERN
                            D   Zu benutzen, wenn ein Dokument sowohl Rutschen als auch Schleudern behandelt

NT SKIDDING (forwards)=   UB RUTSCHEN
NT SKIDDING (sideways)=   UB SCHLEUDERN

SKIDDING (forwards)   = RUTSCHEN
  BT SKIDDING   OB RUTSCHEN +
                              SCHLEUDERN

SKIDDING (sideways)   = SCHLEUDERN
  BT SKIDDING   OB RUTSCHEN +
                              SCHLEUDERN

Example of situation 2

The English phrase 'solar heating' can be expressed in French by the terms *chauffage* and *energie solaire*. Here it is possible, though again deprecated as being even more dangerous than the use of the loan term, to coin a new term, in this case *chauffage solaire*. However, factoring (see E2.4.2) will give a better result and, in this particular situation, can be solved in two ways, depending on the degree of usage of the term 'solar heating'.

Solution (a):
HEATING   = CHAUFFAGE
SOLAR ENERGY   = ENERGIE SOLAIRE

Solar heating
  USE HEATING + SOLAR ENERGY

Solution (b):
SOLAR HEATING = CHAUFFAGE + ENERGIE SOLAIRE
HEATING   = CHAUFFAGE
SOLAR ENERGY   = ENERGIE SOLAIRE

Example of situation 3
The French word *bétail* can be translated into English as livestock which
includes cattle and horses; but the French expression *gros bétail* which
also includes cattle and horses has no clear equivalent in English. Here
there are three solutions (again disregarding the use of loan terms), the
third solution being the combination of the first two.

Solution (a) ignores one pair of generic terms:

GROS BETAIL = CATTLE + HORSES
                        SN Use this combination as an equivalent
                            to the French term GROS BETAIL
                        NT CATTLE
                        NT HORSES

Solution (b) makes the two generic terms synonymous, and selects one
as being equivalent to the generic term in the other language:

BETAIL   = LIVESTOCK
    EP Gros bétail   NT CATTLE
    TS BOEUF   NT HORSES
    TS CHEVAL

Gros bétail
    EM BETAIL

This last situation is clearly one which calls for expert linguistic
assistance, and will not be easily appreciated by the monoglot. In fact,
one reputable dictionary gives *bétail* as being translatable to either cattle
or livestock, *gros bétail* as being only bovine cattle, and a third term,
menu bétail as including sheep and goats. Thus *bétail* can be seen to
either include or exclude horses, and *gros bétail* to definitely exclude
horses.

○ Non-equivalence
What this actually means is that there is no simply expressed equivalent,
and the only two possible solutions are the loan term or the coined term.
In both cases the introduced terms should be accompanied by scope
notes.

In solution (a), the German term is lent to the English thesaurus:

BERUFSVERBOT   = BERUFSVERBOT
                        SN Alleged prohibition of certain
                            classes of persons from official
                            employment. Loan term adopted
                            from German; used only in
                            some political contexts.

In solution (b), a French term is coined as being equivalent to the
English:

STEAM CRACKING   = VAPOCRAQUAGE
                        NE Craquage à la vapeur d'eau.
                            Terme équivalent au terme
                            anglais STEAM CRACKING.

I1.3 Other considerations

In most other aspects the guidelines for multilingual thesaurus compilation follow those for monolingual construction, but there are a few additional points to be made arising from the language problem and from variations in local usage. In all cases, two basic rules obtain: first, try to use the most familiar form of a term and second, cross refer from the others. Thus:

NETHERLANDS   = PAYS-BAS
  UF Holland   EP Hollande

Holland   Hollande
  USE NETHERLANDS   EM PAYS-BAS

While national institutions should appear the same in all versions (e.g. Royal Society), international institutions should be translated and cross-references made from their abbreviations, e.g.

EUROPEAN   = COMMUNAUTES
     COMMUNITIES   EUROPEENNES
  UF EC   EP CE

EC   EM COMMUNAUTES
  USE EUROPEAN   EUROPEENNES
     COMMUNITIES

The conventions governing the use of singulars and plurals may vary between languages. For example, French and German both prefer the singular:

| ANIMALS | ANIMAL | TIER |
| CHILDREN | ENFANT | KIND |

The homograph problem can now occur within one language or between several. The first instance is no different to the problem in monolingual work and is so treated:

TOUR   (bâtiment) = TOWERS
TOUR   (outil)   = LATHES
TOUR   (voyage)   = TOURS
TOUR   (rotation) = ROTATION

The homograph between languages will present a potential problem only if one alphabetical sequence is employed for some reason, and here a simple discriminating code can be used. Where the English/French equivalents are

BEAMS (radiation) = RAYON
RAYON   = SOIE ARTIFICIELLE

confusion can be avoided by using RAYON(E) and RAYON(F).

Finally, the abbreviations for thesaural relationships are given in English, French and German, together with a set of mathematical symbols which, being language-independent, might be preferred.

BT	Broader term	TG	Terme générique	OB	Oberbegriff	<
NT	Narrower term	TS	Terme spécifique	UB	Unterbegriff	>
RT	Related term	VA	Voir aussi	VB	Verwandter Begriff	−
USE	Use	EM	Employer	BS	Benutze	→
UF	Used for	EP	Employé pour	BF	Benutzt für	=
SN	Scope note	NE	Note explicative	D	Definition	

I2. Thesaurus reconciliation and integration

With the proliferation of thesauri, the problem of incompatibility between indexing languages increases. Lack of compatibility hampers not only the transfer of records between systems using diverse controlled languages, but also searching across databases using different thesauri.

The availability of Standards for thesaurus construction has encouraged the development of thesauri with similar structures, but there are still incompatibilities between thesauri. The main differences in thesauri in the same subject field are as follows:

○ Specificity
One system may contain detailed and precise terminology, while another may consist mainly of broad terms.

○ Exhaustivity
One thesaurus may omit some areas of the subject field, while another thesaurus may cover all aspects.

○ Compound terms
One system may use pre-coordinated (i.e., compound) terms where another will express the same concepts by the combination of separate terms. If the thesaurus construction rules were followed closely on this point, the problem of compatibility would not be so common. As has been seen in paragraph E2.4.2(b), rigid commitment to the Standard is not always practicable, and different interpretation of the rules will result.

○ Synonyms
The choice of preferred forms among synonymous or quasi-synonymous concepts differs from thesaurus to thesaurus.

○ Interrelationships
The hierarchies in thesauri may differ in structure and in emphasis. Hierarchical levels occurring in one thesaurus may be absent from another. Associatively related terms are even more subject to change from one thesaurus to another, since inclusion of a relationship may be influenced by the subject interest or viewpoint of the particular organization for which the thesaurus is compiled.

Approaches to the reconciliation of incompatible thesauri include switching systems, merging and integration, and macrothesauri.

I2.1. Switching systems
Switching systems involve the creation of an 'Intermediate Lexicon' to which cooperating indexing languages (classification systems as well as thesauri) may each be reciprocally mapped.

Indexing language A may be switched to indexing languages B, C and D via the Intermediate Lexicon X, and language B to the other three languages, and so on. Research work by Horsnell (39) and Horsnell and Merrett (40) showed that, to be most effective, the Intermediate Lexicon must be as specific as the most detailed language to be switched. The research appeared to show that the retrieval performance of indexing language B switched to language D was as effective in searching the database D as indexing language D itself.

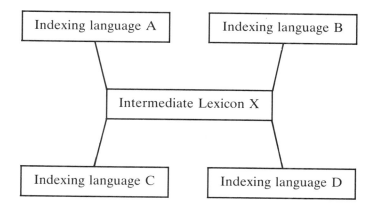

I2.2. Merging and integration

A method of revealing matches and mismatches between thesauri in the same subject field is to merge the terms into one alphabetical sequence. There are two stages of merging. The first brings together matched preferred terms and entry terms in the alphabetical sequence. The second merges into one entry the matched terms and their thesaural relationships to show consistencies and inconsistencies, as in Figure 27. The figure shows an extract from an entry in a proposed descriptor bank consisting of merged thesauri in the social sciences (3–4).

Figure 27. Descriptor bank entry 'Integrated thesaurus of the social sciences'

	* IC	IL	IS	MA	PM	SP	UT
NUPTIALITY							
IC : 22230							
IL : 14.01							
IS : 15421							
MA : 14.02.05							
PM : 13.01.00							
UT : R10.71							
F = Nuptialite		IL	IS	MA	PM		
S = Nupcialidad		IL		MA	PM		
= Marriage rate						SP	
< Population dynamics						SP	
< Population events							UT
– Divorce						SP	
– Families						SP	
– Family system						SP	
– Genetic counselling						SP	
– Marriage	IC	IL	IS	MA	PM		UT
– Nuptiality·rate					PM		
– Nuptiality table					PM		
– Sexual union					PM		
– Statistical data						SP	

* Codes indicating thesauri included in the descriptor bank, e.g. MA = *Macrothesaurus*, UT = *UNESCO thesaurus*.

The descriptor bank would show exact equivalences. For example, six thesauri out of twenty use the term Nuptiality. It also shows inexact and partial equivalences between terms in those thesauri providing this information in the equivalence relation cross-references. For example, thesaurus A may use the term Single women as the preferred term, whereas thesaurus B uses Spinsters. The descriptor bank reveals the equivalence between terms in thesauri A and B through the Use/UF reference code in thesaurus A, which shows Spinsters as equivalent to Single women, even though thesaurus B does not itself have this information.

    SINGLE WOMEN   *[thesaurus A]*
       UF   Spinsters
       BT   Unmarried people
       RT   Bachelors

    SPINSTERS   *[thesaurus B]*
       BT   Unmarried people
       RT   Bachelors

    Spinsters
       USE SINGLE WOMEN   *[thesaurus A]*

The descriptor bank also gives information on the matches and discrepancies between hierarchical and associative relationships in different thesauri. It also brings together definitions, scope notes and foreign language equivalents for the merged terms.

Examples of merged vocabularies developed beyond the design stage are the BRS/TERM database and the Vocabulary Switching System. The BRS/TERM database (45) is an online merged vocabulary of controlled terms in the behavioural and social sciences, which also provides natural language equivalents of the controlled terms. The Vocabulary Switching System (VSS) is an experimental database, developed at Battelle Columbus Laboratories, and described by Niehoff and others (50–53). The field covered by VSS was originally energy and related subjects, but this was extended to four areas: physical sciences, life sciences, social sciences, and business. The number of vocabularies merged was extended from six to fifteen. In the response to the input of a term, the system shows matches in other vocabularies (see Figure 28), ranging from exact matches and synonyms, broader, narrower and related terms, to word matches (i.e., all compound terms and phrases within which the word appears) and word stem matches. An evaluation of the system, described in the final report (51), showed that the merging of vocabularies for online searching had potentially wide appeal, and that the more vocabularies in the same subject areas are included, the better the performance. Performance is also improved if the vocabularies have well-developed relationship structures and if the stemming search options are avoided.

The merging of vocabularies, including thesauri, gives the advantage of an end-product which is richer in terms and relationships than the constituent vocabularies alone. Their use is not limited to controlled language systems. In mixed controlled and natural language systems, merged controlled terms may be used to search in free-text situations.

Figure 28. Vocabulary Switching System

WELCOME TO *VSS* – VOCABULARY SWITCHING SYSTEM
USING BATTELLE'S DATA MANAGEMENT SYSTEM, BASIS

VSS   CONTAINS FOUR VOCABULARY SETS
   1– BUSINESS
      A. ABI   B. MANAGEMENT CONTENTS
   2– BEHAVIOUR SCIENCE
      A. ERIC   B. PSYCH ABSTRACTS
   3– LIFE SCIENCE
      A. BIOSIS   B. CHEM ABSTRACTS
      C. MESH
   4– PHYSICAL SCIENCE
      A. DOE   B. CHEM ABSTRACTS
      C. EI   D. INSPEC
      E. IRON   F. NASA

PLEASE SELECT 1 OF THE 4 VOCABULARY SETS
   BY ENTERING EITHER 1, 2, 3, OR 4

     ? | 4 |

VSS   PROVIDES FOR 6 SWITCHING OPTIONS:
   1– SYNONYMS
   2– BROWSE
   3– NARROWER TERMS
   4– BROADER TERMS
   5– NARROWER/BROADER TERMS
   6– OTHER (USER-DEFINED)

PLEASE SELECT 1 OF THE 6 OPTIONS
   BY ENTERING EITHER 1, 2, 3, 4, 5, OR 6

     ? | 2 |

SPECIFY THE MAXIMUM NUMBER OF TERMS
   TO BE DISPLAYED PER VOCABULARY.
   ENTER A NUMBER.

     ? | 10 |

PLEASE ENTER A SINGLE SEARCH TERM OR COMMAND

    ? <u>HEAVY WATER</u>

SWITCH SUCCESSFUL

TERM TYPE	VOCAB	TERM
YOUR TERM	DOE	HEAVY WATER
YOUR TERM	EI	HEAVY WATER
YOUR TERM	INSPEC	HEAVY WATER
YOUR TERM	NASA	HEAVY WATER
RELATED	DOE	COOLANTS
RELATED	NASA	COOLANTS
RELATED	DOE	DEUTERIUM COMPOUNDS
RELATED	EI	DEUTERIUM COMPOUNDS
RELATED	INSPEC	DEUTERIUM COMPOUNDS
RELATED	NASA	DEUTERIUM COMPOUNDS
RELATED	DOE	MODERATORS
RELATED	CHEM A	MODERATORS
RELATED	INSPEC	MODERATORS
RELATED	NASA	MODERATORS
RELATED	DOE	TRITIUM COMPOUNDS
RELATED	INSPEC	TRITIUM COMPOUNDS
RELATED	DOE	DUAL TEMPERATURE PROCESS
RELATED	DOE	DEUTERIUM
RELATED	EI	DEUTERIUM
RELATED	INSPEC	DEUTERIUM
RELATED	NASA	DEUTERIUM
RELATED	DOE	TRITIUM
RELATED	EI	TRITIUM
RELATED	INSPEC	TRITIUM
RELATED	NASA	TRITIUM
RELATED	INSPEC	FISSION REACTOR MATERIALS
WD MATCH	DOE	HEAVY WATER PLANTS
WD MATCH	DOE	SGHWR REACTOR

The limitation of the merged vocabulary, if it consists of an alphabetical listing of the terms from the constituent indexing languages, is that it does not show concept relationships which the purely verbal approach overlooks. It cannot express inexact and partial equivalences between terms not indicated by the cross-reference structure of the merged vocabularies. For example, the term Aural stimulus in vocabulary A may be close in meaning to Audio stimulus in vocabulary B, but this will go undetected if there are no entries in the synonym or related term fields of either term to show the link between them. A method of discovering these equivalencies is to plot the terms of the merged thesauri against a well-structured master classification, as suggested in the design study for the 'Integrated thesaurus of the social sciences' (3). This would bring terms with similar meanings together at the same class number, where the links between them would become apparent as the fields were analysed. The TERM database is also concerned with the concept approach to vocabulary merging. Instead of a master classification, there is a series of small subject areas, known as 'titles', covering, for example, 'Poverty areas' or 'Battered women'. (See Figure 29.) Controlled terms and free-text terms which are relevant to this area are gathered under the concept heading. The intellectual intervention of the compiler is an important factor in this type of concept-oriented merged vocabulary.

Figure 29. Vocabulary database for searchers TERM record

```
TI  SPOUSE ABUSE.
ER  CONSIDER: BATTERED-WOMEN.
ME  SPOUSE-ABUSE.
NC  (090A.CC. = SPOUSE ABUSE).
PS  FAMILY-VIOLENCE. (1982 + ).
SO  CONSIDER: ABUSE. (001050). BATTERED. (051240). (ANDED TO). WIFE.
    (489880). WOMAN (490000).
FT  SPOUSE ABUSE. BATTERED WOMEN. WIFE BEATING. WIFE ASSAULT. WIFE
    RAPE. ABUSED SPOUSES. ABUSED WOMEN. WIFE BATTERING. WIFE ABUSE.
    CONJUGAL CRIME. WIFEBEATING. SPOUSE ASSAULT. BATTERED HUSBAND.
    VIOLENT HOME. FAMILY VIOLENCE. BATTERED WIFE. BATTERED WIVES.
    BEATEN WOMEN. DOMESTIC VIOLENCE. HUSBAND ABUSE. ABUSIVE HUSBANDS.
    MOTHERS IN STRESS. WOMEN IN CRISIS. VICTIM OF ABUSE BY MATE.
    BATTERED WIFE SYNDROME. VERBAL SPOUSE ABUSE. WIFE BATTERER.
    MENTAL CRUELTY. MARITAL RAPE.
```

KEY TO PARAGRAPH LABELS ABOVE:

TI Title	**ME** MeSH Descriptor	**SO** Sociological Abstracts Descriptors
ER ERIC Descriptor	**NC** Family Resources Code	
	PS PsycINFO Descriptor	**FT** Free Text Terms

I2.3. Macrothesauri and microthesauri

A microthesaurus is a specialized thesaurus that maps onto, and is entirely included within, the hierarchical structure of some broader thesaurus, the macrothesaurus. The macrothesaurus may be published as a broad subject thesaurus, separate from the microthesauri which are compatible with it, or it may be available with the broad macrothesaurus structure and the detailed microthesauri combined in one system.

A more detailed survey of compatibility and convertibility of thesauri is found in Chapter 19 of Lancaster's *Vocabulary control for information retrieval* (46).

I3. The searching thesaurus

If, in a computerized system, the expense of indexing cannot be justified, vocabulary aids will be needed to supplement the search aids already available (for example, truncation, and word distance indication). These vocabulary aids vary from the simple to the sophisticated.

○ Database term listings
These are alphabetical listings of significant words in the database, with an indication of frequency, but no attempt to show relationships.

○ Synonym listings
These are lists of terms and their equivalents which may be substituted for the term in an online search.

○ Hedges
These are fragments of search strategies, saved for subsequent use. Hedges or Search Facets (48), usually consist of a number of terms with 'or' listings. These search strategies need to be indexed and cross-referenced so as to be located when required.

○ Conventional thesauri – enhanced
Conventional thesauri may be used in searching any natural language database, covering the same subject areas. Several thesauri and not one only may be employed. Both the preferred and non-preferred terms in these thesauri may be used in the search. Conventional thesauri with permuted indexes and hierarchical and systematic displays help to speed access to relevant terms. Conventional thesauri may be enhanced for natural language searching by increasing the number of terms leading to the nearest appropriate preferred term.

○ Merged thesauri
Merged and integrated thesauri (see I2) present a richer choice of terminology and display of term interrelationships than the individual vocabularies alone, and are likely to be useful aids in natural language searches, especially, as in the case of the BRS/TERM database, where free indexing terms are given in addition to the merged thesaurus terms. This system, implemented by BRS (45), includes five social science thesauri, including the *Thesaurus of ERIC descriptors* and the *Thesaurus of psychological terms*. The data is displayed under concepts (known as 'titles'), such as History, and Poverty Areas. Under each

concept are arranged indexing terms and equivalent, broader, narrower and related terms of the constituent thesauri, followed by a possible list of free-text terms (FT) for the concept (see Figure 29).

The character of the searching thesaurus, also known as the post-controlled thesaurus (46, Chapter 17), is in the process of evolving. It is likely to differ from the conventional indexing thesaurus in the following points:

○ It is not used in indexing, except where the same thesaurus functions as a conventional thesaurus as well as a search aid in combined natural and controlled language systems.

○ The accommodation of new terms is not as urgent in a thesaurus used only in searching as it is in an indexing thesaurus, where a speedy decision has to be made by the thesaurus maintenance staff so as not to delay the work of the indexers.

○ The thesaurus need not be the sole indexing language available to the searcher – other published thesauri, subject heading lists and classification systems, dictionaries, encyclopaedias, etc. may also be used as supplementary tools.

○ The form of the searching thesaurus may not be unlike that of the conventional thesaurus, but may have additional features, such as:

- considerably enlarged entry vocabularies;
- the ability to index and cross-reference the stored 'hedge' searches;
- merged terms from several thesauri, enhanced with free-text terms, as in the BRS/TERM database.

More detailed information on search vocabularies and thesauri may be found in Lancaster (46, Chapter 17) and in a paper by Piternick (57).

Section J   *Construction techniques*

In this section a step-by-step approach to thesaurus construction (subsequent to checking that a thesaurus is required – see B1) is given with illustrations from a hypothetical thesaurus.

The reader is referred for further information to three publications which also include practical steps in thesaurus construction, namely Townley and Gee (68), Orna (55) and Soergel (64).

J1. Definition of subject field

As a first step, the subject field is defined, the boundaries of the subject are established, and a distinction is made between those parts which must be treated in depth and those of marginal importance. (See also J7.1: preliminary organization of the subject field.)

J2. Selection of thesaurus characteristics and layout

By this stage the compiler should have clarified his or her ideas as to what type of thesaurus is to be constructed, having already studied the overall system requirements (B2–B3), and should now know whether controlled language only, natural language alone, or a hybrid system of natural and controlled language is to be used. The compiler should know if the thesaurus is to serve as a macrothesaurus, a switching language, or a searching thesaurus for a natural language system. A decision should have been made on features of the thesaurus, such as specificity, compound terms and the use of auxiliary precision devices. The compiler should also know how the thesaurus is to be presented, that is, whether there is to be a graphical or a systematic display as well as an alphabetical display. In the case of the hypothetical thesaurus (on Catering) used here to illustrate construction techniques, it is assumed that a decision has been made that the thesaurus is to serve the needs of a database with controlled and natural language. It is to have a medium level of specificity and term pre-coordination, but with no auxiliary precision devices, such as weights. The preferred layout could be a systematic display supported by a full alphabetical thesaurus as in the BSI *ROOT thesaurus* (H3.3.3), though other options discussed in Section H, Thesaurus display, would be possible following the same construction steps. These options include an alphabetical display with single or multiple hierarchies (H1) accompanied by broad subject groups (H3.1) or graphic displays (H4).

J3. Notification of intent

When the decision is made to produce a new thesaurus for eventual publication, notification of intent should be announced in an appropriate professional journal. In the United Kingdom, the Aslib Information Resources Centre should also be informed. To ensure entry in the database and guide of the Commission of the European Communities (see B3.1), details should be sent to the Gesellschaft für Information und Dokumentation (GID) at Frankfurt.

J4. Deductive versus inductive method

If a thesaurus is compiled using the deductive method, the examination of selected terms to find structure and to introduce vocabulary control is delayed until a sufficient number of terms have been collected. In contrast, if the inductive method is used, terms are admitted to the thesaurus and are used in indexing as soon as they are encountered in the literature. Vocabulary control is applied from the outset and the terms are allocated to one or more broader categories. Indexing is started earlier in the project, but there may have to be revision of the indexing at a later stage when the significance of the terms used is better appreciated.

In the steps outlined below, the deductive method is favoured, although some vocabulary control is applied early, as the controlled form of terms is recorded on the initial record forms during term collection, whenever this is possible, and terms are allocated to one or more of several broad subject fields, or facets, for later analysis. The terms would not be used for 'live' indexing until all relationships had been established, form and choice of term finalized, and the resulting thesaurus tested.

J5. Selection of terms

The task of assembling terms starts as soon as the subject field is defined. There are three main written sources of terminology: terms in standardized form, non-standardized terminology found in the literature, and terminology in users' recorded questions and profiles. The two unwritten sources are the knowledge and experience of users and experts, and the similar resources of the compiler.

J5.1. Terminological sources in standardized form

○ Thesauri and lists of terms
These will include specialized thesauri and term lists and the appropriate sections of general thesauri. Thesauri are a source of synonyms, broader, narrower and related terms, and to a lesser extent, definitions. (For details of thesaurus bibliographies see B3.1.)

○ Classification schedules
These include specialized schemes and the appropriate sections of general schemes such as the Universal Decimal Classification, the Library of Congress Classification, and BC2. Classification schemes may

lack the word form control and precise display of relationships necessary for a thesaurus, but may be rich in terminology. The Bliss Classification (see also F4) includes many synonyms and some definitions as well as hierarchies of terms. (Some of the bibliographies of thesauri mentioned in B3.1 also include details of classification systems.)

If there are a large number of small vocabularies and thesauri in the subject field, it might be useful to merge these, so that the terms they contain may be viewed more easily by scanning a single list. Such an operation, however, will almost certainly require computing facilities.

○ Encyclopaedias, lexicons, dictionaries, glossaries
These may be universal or discipline-oriented, monolingual, bilingual, or multilingual. They may be alphabetically organized or concept-oriented (i.e. arranged systematically under concepts).

Always check that it is the latest edition that is being searched.

○ Terminological databanks
Terminological databanks are another source of thesaurus terms. Databanks provide definitions, synonyms, and sometimes broader, narrower and related terms.

○ Treatises on the terminology of a subject field

○ Indexes of journals and abstract journals

○ Indexes of other publications in the field

J5.2. Literature scanning
In all subject fields, and in particular in those which are developing rapidly, it is not sufficient to rely solely on 'pre-arranged' sources for term selection. The literature must be scanned for non-standardized, free-text terms. The literature scanned should not be limited to monographs and journal articles but should extend to reports, pamphlets, product catalogues, conference papers, patent specifications, and standards.

J5.2.1. Manual selection
In manual selection, cards should be used to record terms and phrases considered significant. If a note is also kept on the card of the number of times that the term occurs in the literature, this will give an indication of the relative importance of the term. If clerical help is available, the compiler may underline the selected terms ready for typing on to cards or (preferably) on to a word processor or microcomputer to produce a machine-readable master file, from which may be produced lists in alphabetical order and also in descending order of frequency of occurrence. The frequency list will assist not only in suggesting the leading candidate terms, but also in the choice of preferred terms among synonyms.

J5.2.2. Automatic term selection
In automatic selection, lists of words are derived by computer from the title, abstracts and full text of documents, where available (see Gilchrist (36, p. 38), and Lancaster (46, Chapter 4)). Ranked lists of most

frequently used terms and phrases are output. Information on the frequency of co-occurrence of terms or phrases with other terms or phrases may also be derived, using statistical techniques. This provides guidance on term groupings and relationships.

J5.3. Question scanning

Terms found in questions put to the system have equal importance as candidates for the thesaurus as those taken from the literature. The questions should be collected from users (see J5.4) or from records of questions, searches, and profiles already encountered. Analysis of user queries on a full-scale research project basis might be considered. This was done as a preliminary step before the 'Community information classification' (80) was compiled. Several thousands of user profiles, held in a large number of community information and advice organizations in the United Kingdom, were computer-analysed to show frequency of term use and co-occurence of subjects.

J5.4. Users'/experts' experience and knowledge

The compiler should seek the advice and cooperation of users and user groups in term selection at all stages of compilation. At the stage of term gathering, users' opinions are invaluable. Compilation through a committee of experts may not be very satisfactory, but advice may be obtained in a more informal manner. Some suggestions as to how to go about this are listed below.

○ Experts may be asked to assist in the scanning of the literature, indexing items with those terms they consider most appropriate.

○ Experts may be asked to list terms of importance in their subject fields.

○ Experts may be asked to list typical questions which they might put to the system.

○ Experts may be shown lists of terms or draft classification schemes, in their own subject fields, and asked to comment, make amendments and add terms.

○ Groups of experts may be asked to discuss the terminology and classification in subject areas which appear difficult to delineate and which require careful clarification.

J5.5. The compiler's experience and knowledge

The compiler's knowledge of the subject and familiarity with the terminology is an asset in term selection and rejection, but it is unwise for the compiler to rely on his or her own knowledge and memory to the exclusion of all other sources.

J6. Recording of the terms

It has already been suggested (J5.2.1) that a record (see Figure 30) should be kept of the terms selected on cards or, preferably, in machine-readable form. Information about the term might include definitions, synonyms, hierarchical and associative relations. In addition, the source of the term might be included; also its frequency of occurrence, and a field for entering a class number, code or broad subject heading to be used in the initial sorting of terms into subject

Figure 30. Term record form

Term CATERING EQUIPMENT	Notation R/Z
UF Kitchen equipment	SN
BT Domestic appliances	Includes food mixers, cooking-ware, tableware etc.
NT Cookers Microwave ovens	Frequency 8
RT	Source Journal articles BSI ROOT Thesaurus Library catalogue

groups for the process of finding structure. When selecting thesaural relationships from existing thesauri care should be taken not to record relationships which would be inappropriate for the particular bias of the thesaurus under construction. In any case some of these recorded relationships may be modified or discarded when the terms are analysed, in relation to the other selected terms, during later construction processes.

J7. Finding structure

J7.1. Preliminary organization of the subjects covered by the thesaurus

Before or during the period of term collection, the subjects covered by the thesaurus should be organized into main categories so that terms, on selection, may be sorted and filed under appropriate headings to await further analysis. This operation is necessary whether a systematic, graphic or solely alphabetical display is the goal, because it will reveal the coverage of the thesaurus, existence of gaps and overloaded areas, and, at the same time, by bringing like terms together, will facilitate the determination of their structural relationships.

The subject coverage of thesauri varies from the broad in scope to the limited and highly specific. Some thesauri are concerned with the whole of knowledge, although usually from a particular viewpoint, or with large sub-sections, such as the Social Sciences or Technology. Other thesauri treat major disciplines, for example Physics, Medicine, Education, or Economics, while many are involved with narrower subject areas such as Microbiology, Welding, Industrial relations, or Drug dependence. In most thesauri, apart from the very general, it is possible to discern at least one and usually several main subject areas which form the core of the thesaurus. Surrounding the core area will be marginal subjects, including common terms such as Geographic areas and Form of document and peripheral subjects which may be required to further define and supplement the terms in the main part of the thesaurus.

Having determined the main and subordinate areas of the thesaurus it must next be decided whether the primary division of the subject area is to be by discipline or subject field or by fundamental facets. It is more usual to divide first by discipline or subject field and then by facets within the subject fields and disciplines, as described in F4 above. There are, however, exceptions. The *Construction industry thesaurus*, for example, is divided by the fundamental facets Time, Place, Properties and Measures, Agents (Persons and Equipment), Operations and Processes, Materials, and Entities (i.e. Parts of Construction Works and Construction Works). An advantage of a subject area partitioned initially by basic facets is that the arrangement may date more slowly than one organized by disciplines or subject fields. On the debit side, concepts expected to be found together in traditional groupings are separated.

There are differences between thesauri organized by disciplines and those arranged by subject field, but these are difficult to analyse. Discipline-based thesauri tend to group subjects according to academic consensus and to emphasize the study aspect, whereas the subject-field-based thesauri concentrate on the phenomena studied and may separate categories which might be closely associated in academic curricula. In practice the two systems overlap, with the subject-field-oriented thesaurus including some disciplines, and vice versa. The consistent use of commonly accepted disciplines is more usual in thesauri covering several fields of knowledge or for the classification of peripheral subject areas. Disciplines may also be preferred in thesauri covering well-defined, traditional subjects, where users would expect to find concepts grouped along familiar lines. If a discipline-oriented thesaurus is to be designed, the *Broad System of Ordering* (82) is a useful source of structure, as is BC2 (97).

For the purpose of illustrating construction techniques it is supposed that a thesaurus is required for a database concerned with catering and related subjects. The scope of this field is wide ranging, but the areas of major and minor importance might be determined as follows:

Core area:	Catering
Closely related areas:	Household technologies
	Hotel management
	Home economics
	Cleaning technologies
	Food technology
Peripheral areas:	All other areas of knowledge in outline, but in more detail Psychology, Education, Law, Medicine, and other related Technologies.
General concepts:	Geographical areas, etc.

In this Catering Thesaurus, the primary organization might be as shown in Figure 31, where the core field of Catering occurs at the end of a sequence of classes which begins with General Concepts, including

Figure 31. Broad subject categories
Catering and related fields

General concepts

Geographical areas
Research, design and testing
Standardization
Management
Organizations

Peripheral subjects

Communication and information
  Computers
Philosophy
Mathematical sciences
Sciences
  Physical sciences
  Earth sciences
  Biology
Agriculture, Food production
Technology and Engineering
  including Construction
Biomedical sciences, Medicine
  Nutrition, Dietetics
  Environmental health
    Food hygiene
  Health services
    Hospitals
Psychology
Education
Social sciences
  Sociology
  Social problems and Welfare
  Politics and Government
    Armed forces
  Law
  Humanities, History, Religion
Arts, literature, leisure

Closely related subjects

Food technology
Household technologies
  Cleaning technology
  Corporate housekeeping
    Hotel management
  Home economics

Catering

Figure 32. Allocation of terms to broad subject categories
Catering and related fields

General concepts
...
Management
    Catering management
    Catering managers
    Financial management
    Office management
    Personnel management
    Planning
    Purchasing
    Recruitment
    Work measurement

Peripheral subjects
...
Psychology
    Attitude
    Conflict
    Interpersonal relations
    Social interaction
    Stress

Education

    Colleges of further education
    Colleges of higher education
    Curricula
    Educational courses
    In-service training
    Polytechnics
    Practical training
    Schools
    Teachers
    Teaching
    Training
    Universities

etc.

Geographical areas, Research, Design, and Testing. Next come the peripheral subjects, organized into disciplines, and subject fields most closely related to Catering, for example Food technology, Household technologies, Cleaning, Hotel management, and Home economics. The final section is concerned with the subject of Catering itself. All the terms occurring in the fields preceding Catering may be used to further qualify the Catering terms. For example, Training from the Education category may be used in combination with the term Waiters, to represent the concept of Training of Waiters, or Engineering maintenance from the Engineering category may be used with Cookers to represent the concept of Maintenance of cookers.

J7.2. Analysis and grouping of terms within broad categories
Terms should be allocated to the appropriate broad category, and arranged within these, initially in alphabetical order (see Figure 32).

J7.2.1. Analysis using a systematic display
Each broad category should be taken in turn and its terms analysed in relation to the other terms in the category to find a structural pattern. For example, supposing the Catering section of the Catering Thesaurus is to be analysed, the first step would be to recognize the basic facets (see F4). These might be, as shown at step A in Figure 33, Personnel, Equipment, Operations (Management, Food preparation, Food service), Areas (Restaurants, Kitchens, etc.), Food and Meals, and Applications (Hospital catering, etc.). Next, the terms within each facet are analysed into hierarchies and families showing subordinate terms indented under their superordinate terms (see step B, Fig. 33). Both hierarchical and associative relationships may be indicated by indenting, for example Catering equipment (related term) and Catering operations (narrower term) are shown in the display as indented one space under the superordinate term Catering. The hierarchical and associative relations are distinguished by an NT or RT, written in the margin against the term, marking its relation to the term one step above. The display is written out, showing indenting and indicating the start of a new characteristic of division, or facet, by a facet indicator (or node label) in parenthesis, preceding the array of terms.

Example:

```
        Catering

        . (Equipment)          ⟵── Facet indicator
(RT)    . Catering equipment    ⎫
(NT)    . . Cooking appliances  ⎬── Indented terms,
(NT)    . . . Cookers           ⎪     coded (NT) and (RT)
(NT)    . . . Microwave ovens   ⎭
```

The use of classificatory techniques gives several benefits. By the grouping of terms, synonyms and near synonyms are brought together and their relationships more easily recognized. For example, in the Food group, the terms Convenience food and Fast food appear. Although these terms are not exact synonyms, in a small thesaurus it may be acceptable to treat them as such and to lead Fast food into Convenience food. The same treatment might be acceptable for the closely related Cooks and Chefs, giving preference to the latter. Classification also shows missing hierarchical levels. For example, Cookers and Microwave ovens brought together in the Catering

Figure 33. Subject field analysis and thesaurus derivation
Catering and related fields

Step A

Find facets/groups
(Arrangement of terms previously listed alphabetically under Catering)

CATERING
(Personnel – general)
Catering personnel

(Equipment)
Catering quipment
Cookers
Microwave ovens

(Operations and personnel associated)
Catering management
Catering managers
Cookery
Chefs
Cooks
Food purchasing
Food preparation
Food service
Waiters
Waiting

(Areas and associated operations)
Bars (licensed)
Canteens
Cafes
Kitchens
Restaurant management
Restaurants

(Food and meals)
Bakery products
Beverages
Convenience food
Dairy products
Fast food
Fish
Food
Food dishes
Fruit
Meals
Menus
Vegetables

Step B

Make hierarchies/arrays
Code terms NT/RT to term one step above

CATERING
(Personnel)
(RT) Catering personnel

(Equipment)
(RT) Catering equipment
(NT) Cooking appliances
(NT) Cookers
(NT) Microwave ovens

(Operations)
Catering operations
(NT) Catering management
(Personnel)
(RT) Catering managers
(NT) Food purchasing
(NT) Food preparation
(Personnel)
(RT) Chefs
(Operations)
(NT) Cookery
(NT) Food service
(NT) Waiting
(Personnel)
(RT) Waiters

(Areas)
(RT) Catering areas
(NT) Bars (licensed)
(NT) Canteens
(NT) Restaurants
(Management)
(RT) Restaurant management
(NT) Kitchens

(Food and meals)
(RT) Food
(Dishes)
(NT) Food dishes
(By special properties)
(NT) Convenience food

Step C

Add SNs, UFs and BT/NT/RTs from other subject fields, and links within the catering field

CATERING
(Personnel)
(RT) Catering personnel
NT **Catering managers**
    Chefs
    Waiters

(Equipment)
(RT) Catering equipment
SN **Includes food mixers, cooking ware, tableware, etc.**
UF **Kitchen equipment**
RT **Dishwashers**
(NT) Cooking appliances
BT **Domestic appliances**
(NT) Cookers
(NT) Microwave ovens

(Operations)
(NT) Catering operations
(NT) Catering management
BT **Management**
NT **Restaurant management**
RT **Food purchasing**

(Personnel)
(RT) Catering managers
BT **Catering personnel**
BT **Managers**

(NT) Food purchasing
BT **Purchasing**
RT **Catering management**

Food preparation
(Personnel)
(RT) Chefs
UF **Cooks**
BT **Catering personnel**
(Operations)
(NT) Cookery

Step D

Make conventional alphabetical display. (A few selected entries. See Figure 36 for complete thesaurus)

CATERING PERSONNEL
NT Catering managers
    Chefs
    Waiters
RT Catering

COOKING APPLIANCES
BT Catering equipment
    Domestic appliances
NT Cookers
    Microwave ovens

CATERING MANAGEMENT
BT Catering operations
    Management
NT Restaurant management
RT Catering managers
    Food purchasing

CHEFS
UF Cooks
BT Catering personnel
RT Food preparation

(Not further analysed)
Educational catering
Hospital catering
Hotel catering
Institutional catering
School catering

(RT) Beverages
(NT) Meat
(NT) Fish
(NT) Dairy products
(NT) Fruit
(NT) Vegetables
(NT) Bakery products
(RT) Meals
(RT) Menus

FOOD SERVICE
(NT) Waiting
(Personnel)
(RT) Waiters
   BT Catering personnel

(Areas)
(RT) Catering areas
(NT) Bars (licensed)
   RT Licensing laws
(NT) Canteens
(NT) Restaurants
(Management)
   Restaurant management
(RT) **BT Catering management**
   Kitchens

(Food and meals)
(RT) Food
(Dishes)
(NT) Food dishes
   RT Meals

(By special properties)
(NT) Convenience food
   UF Fast food

(Individual foods)
(RT) Beverages
   UF Drinks
(NT) Meat
(NT) Fish
(NT) Dairy products
(NT) Fruit
(NT) Vegetables
(NT) Bakery products
(RT) Meals
   RT Food dishes
(RT) Menus
   RT Diet

FOOD SERVICE
   BT Catering operations
   NT Waiting

BARS (licensed)
   BT Catering areas
   RT Licensing laws

RESTAURANT MANAGEMENT
   BT Catering management
   RT Restaurants

FOOD DISHES
   RT Food
   Meals

BEVERAGES
   UF Drinks
   RT Food

MEALS
   RT Catering
   Food dishes
   Menus

equipment facet suggests a common broader term Cooking appliances, and the assembling of terms such as Food preparation, Food purchasing and Food service in another group suggests the generic term Catering Operations. Classification may also show gaps in hierarchies. For example, the Catering areas facet in Figure 33 includes Canteens, Restaurants, Bars, and Kitchens, and it is easy to check what similar areas are missing. Snack bars and Dining-rooms are not represented, and might be added.

Figure 33 shows that the next step (step C) is to add details of scope notes (see D5.2) and equivalence relationships (see F1), which may have already been noted on the term record.

Examples:

[Scope note]

Catering equipment
   SN Includes Food mixers, cooking ware, tableware etc.

[Equivalence relationship]

Catering equipment
   UF Kitchen equipment

Also to be added are polyhierarchies (see F2.4) and related terms occurring in other subject fields or in different facets and arrays of the same field (see F3.3.2). Again, some of the information may be shown on the term record made at the time of term selection.

Examples:

[Polyhierarchies]

Cooking appliances
   BT Domestic appliances

where Cooking appliances, in the display, is shown in the Catering field, although it is also a narrower term to the broader concept, Domestic appliances, located in the display for the Household technologies section.

[Associatively related terms]

 Menus
   RT Diet

where Diet is under Dietetics in the Medical field.

Food dishes
   RT Meals

Meals
   RT Food dishes

where Food dishes and Meals are both in Catering, but separated in the display.

When the Household technology and Medical sections are analysed, reciprocal entries will be made.

Example:

Domestic appliances
   NT Cooking appliances

Diet
   RT Menus

Each subject field must be analysed in the same way as the Catering field. This means that the terms are grouped into facets and within these, arrays and hierarchies are developed. Terms which are related terms in the arrays are coded RT to distinguish them from those coded NT, the narrower terms. Lastly, scope notes, equivalent terms and broader, narrower and related terms in other parts of the display are added to the terms as appropriate.

When all this detail is assembled for each subject field, sufficient information is available for the derivation of a conventional alphabetical thesaurus from the display as seen in step D of Figure 33, whether this work is done manually or by computer. (Conventional thesaurus generation from a systematic display is discussed fully in J8.1.)

J7.2.2. Analysis using a graphic display

An alternative method of analysing the subject field is to use family tree structures, PRECIS-type networks, arrowgraphs, or terminographs to give a graphic presentation of structure and relationships (see H4). For example, the relationships in the *ISDD thesaurus* (see H4.1) were found through the development of tree structures. If arrowgraphs are compiled as illustrated in Figure 34, facet analysis may be used to determine structure. Facets are displayed together and their arrays indicated by connecting arrows. Associative relationships within the same arrowgraph are indicated either by the code RT (for example, against the term Catering equipment, showing it is not hierarchically related to the main term Catering), or by a dotted line connecting the related terms, as between Food purchasing and Catering management. Relationships (BT/NT/RT) with terms in other arrowgraphs are indicated by slashed and dotted lines leading to the reference number of the appropriate chart. Equivalence relationships (UF) are given beneath the preferred terms. A conventional alphabetical thesaurus may be derived from the display, and published with or without the accompanying arrowgraphs. If the display and arrowgraph is printed, the coded RTs and the UFs could be omitted to increase the clarity of the layout. The box chart or terminograph display method (H4.3) may also be used during the construction process to display facets, hierarchies and interrelationships within subject fields.

J7.3. Editing the systematic display

If the systematic display in Figure 33 is to be printed out as part of the thesaurus, it must be edited. This consists of adding a notation (see F5), selecting typefaces, checking the cross-references and adding notation to these (see Figure 35). When choosing typefaces it is useful to know that changes in typeface and size may replace indenting to indicate levels of the three or four highest terms in the hierarchies.

Example:

Indenting	Typeface change
Catering	**CATERING**
Catering equipment	**Catering equipment**
Cooking appliances	Cooking appliances
Cookers	Cookers

Figure 34. Arrowgraph as a construction tool

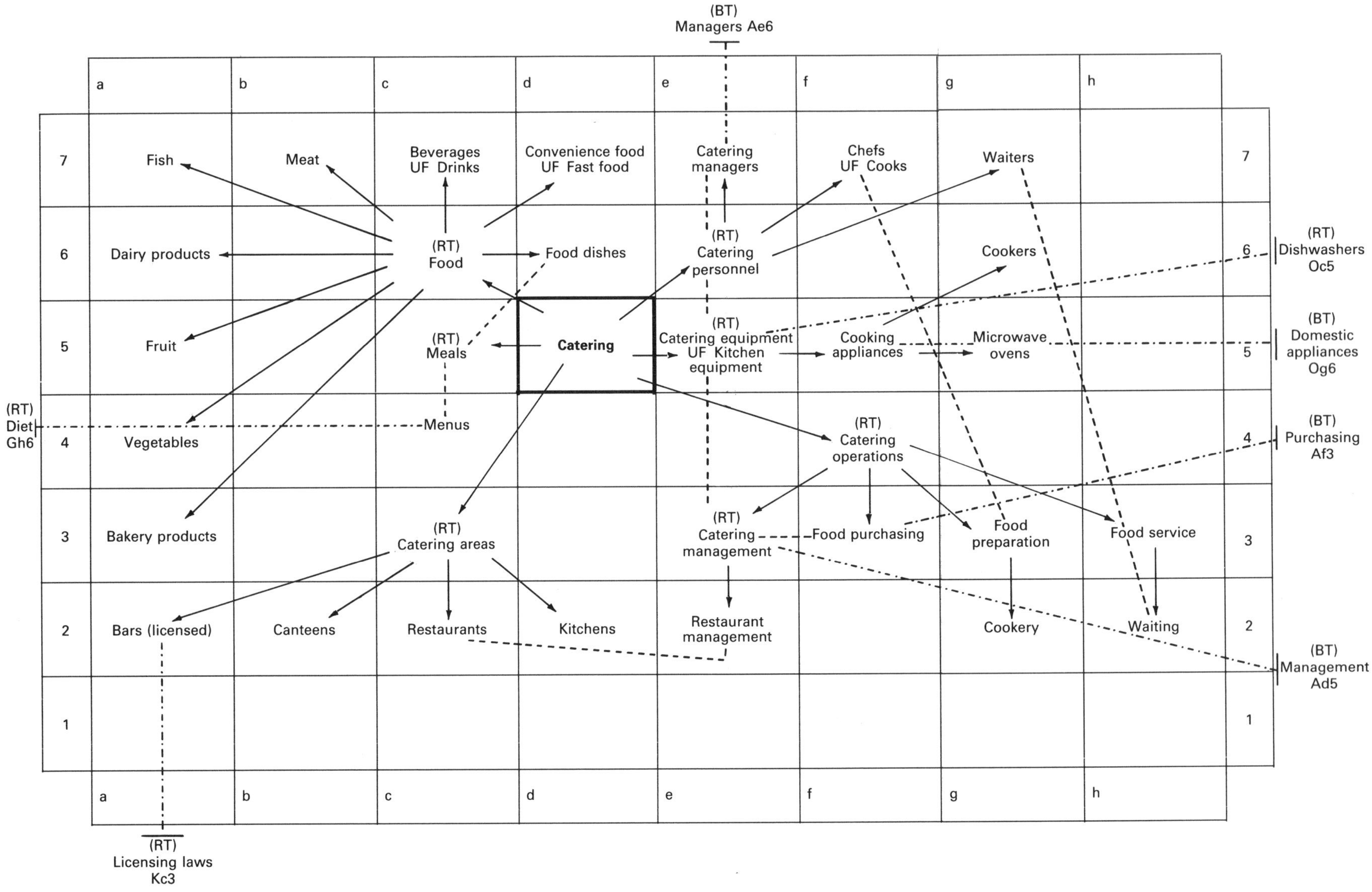

It is assumed that it has been decided to use the BSI *ROOT thesaurus* style display which shows polyhierarchies in one preferred place with reciprocal references between the non-preferred and the preferred location (see H3.3.3). For example, the preferred place for Cooking appliances is SJ under Catering equipment and not under Domestic appliances OAD in the Household technologies section (see Figure 35), and Food purchasing TF is placed under Catering operations rather than under Purchasing at AMQ. Catering managers TAB, Chefs THB, and Waiters TPD.B, are placed with the operations with which they are associated (that is Catering management TA, Food preparation TH and Waiting TPD) rather than under Catering personnel RB. This relationship between Personnel and Operation is associative (RT) and not hierarchical, and introduces a mixed associative/hierarchical relationship, in which the term Waiter, for instance, has one broader term in the display Catering personnel, and one related term Waiting TPD which is selected as the preferred place. The same applies to Restaurant management at UMA for which the preferred place is under the 'entity managed', Restaurants UM, with which it is associatively related and not under its broader term Catering management TA. The term Restaurant management would not be admitted, if the factoring rules were strictly adhered to (E2.4.2), but it is assumed that in this particular database, the concept is of sufficient importance to warrant an exception.

As may be seen in Figure 35, cross-references are made between the term and its polyhierarchies elsewhere in the display, using the code *BT and *NT.

Example:

SJ	Cooking appliances	
	*BT Domestic appliances	OAD
OAD	Domestic appliances	
	*NT Cooking appliances	SJ
TPD.B	Waiters	
	*BT Catering personnel	RB
RB	Catering personnel	
	*NT Waiters	TPD.B

Reciprocals of associatively related terms are cross-referenced using the code *RT.

Example:

TA	Catering management	
	*RT Food purchasing	TF
TF	Food purchasing	
	*RT Catering management	TA
UE	Bars (licensed)	
	*RT Licensing laws	KNF
KNF	Licensing laws	
	*RT Bars (licensed)	UE

All these relationships have to be carefully checked and the corresponding notation added. In a large thesaurus this operation is best handled by computer.

**Figure 35. Systematic display (catering and related subjects)
edited for printing and alphabetical derivation**

AM	**Management**
	*NT Catering management TA
	(Personnel)
AMB *(RT)*	Managers
	*NT Catering managers TAB
	…
	(Operations)
	…
AMQ *(RT)*	Purchasing
	*NT Food purchasing TF
	…
K	**Law**
	…
KNF	Licensing laws
	*RT Bars (licensed) UE
	…
O	**Household technologies**
	…
OAD *(RT)*	Domestic appliances
	*NT Cooking appliances SJ
	…
OC	Cleaning technology
	(Equipment)
OCD *(RT)*	Cleaning equipment
OCD.F	Dishwashers
	*RT Catering equipment S
	…
R	**Catering**
	(Personnel)
RB *(RT)*	Catering personnel
	*NT Catering managers TAB
	Chefs THB
	Waiters TPD.B
	(Equipment)
S *(RT)*	Catering equipment
	SN Includes food mixers,
	cooking ware, tableware, etc.

	Catering (cont.)
	Catering equipment (cont.)
	UF Kitchen equipment
	*RT Dishwashers OCD.F
SJ	Cooking appliances
	*BT Domestic appliances OAD
SJC	Cookers
SJK	Microwave ovens
	(Operations)
T *(RT)*	Catering operations
TA	Catering management
	*BT Management AM
	*NT Restaurant management UMA
	*RT Food purchasing TF
	(Personnel)
TAB *(RT)*	Catering managers
	*BT Catering personnel RB
	Managers AMB
TF	Food purchasing
	*BT Purchasing AMQ
	*RT Catering management TA
TH	Food preparation
	(Personnel)
THB *(RT)*	Chefs
	UF Cooks
	*BT Catering personnel RB
	(Operations)
THG	Cookery
TP	Food service
TPD	Waiting
	(Personnel)
TPD.B (RT)	Waiters
	*BT Catering personnel RB
	(Areas)
U	Catering areas
UE	Bars (licensed)
	*RT Licensing laws KNF
UH	Canteens
UM	Restaurants
	(Management)
UMA *(RT)*	Restaurant management
	*BT Catering management TA
UR	Kitchens

J8. Alphabetical thesaurus production from a systematic display

The subject display in systematic form as shown in Figure 33 may be used to produce a conventional alphabetical thesaurus (see H1.1) or variations of the alphabetical thesaurus such as the multilevel thesaurus (see H1.2). Equally, as will be seen, it may be used to produce a thesaurus with a systematic display and a full alphabetical thesaurus, or a systematic thesaurus with an index only.

J8.1. Conventional alphabetical thesaurus production
The information in the systematic display in Figure 33 is re-arranged in the standard alphabetical thesaurus format. (See Figure 36 for a full thesaurus derived from the terms in the Catering Section.)

Example (a): Details in the systematic display

Catering

(Equipment)

(RT) Catering equipment		*[Coded RT to superordinate Catering term]*
	SN Includes food mixers, cooking ware, tableware etc.	
	UF Kitchen equipment	*[Equivalent term. Needs USE entry]*
	RT Dishwashers	*[Additional RT]*
(NT)	Cooking appliances	*[Indented term – NT]*
	BT Domestic appliances	*[Additional BT]*
(NT)	Cookers	*[Indented term – NT]*
(NT)	Microwave ovens	*[Indented term – NT]*

Example (b): Conventional alphabetical thesaurus

(Entries for Catering Equipment and Cooking Appliances)

CATERING EQUIPMENT
SN   Includes food mixers, cooking ware, tableware etc.
UF   Kitchen equipment
NT   Cooking appliances   *[Note that the BT/NTs are to one level only]*
RT   Catering
       Dishwashers

COOKING APPLIANCES
BT   Catering equipment
       Domestic appliances
NT   Cookers
       Microwave ovens

(Reciprocals, excluding the term Catering)

Kitchen equipment
   USE CATERING EQUIPMENT

DISHWASHERS
  RT   Catering equipment

DOMESTIC APPLIANCES
  NT   Catering equipment

COOKERS
  BT   Cooking appliances

MICROWAVE OVENS
  BT   Cooking appliances

If preferred, the thesaurus may be in the form of a multilevel display.

Example:

CATERING EQUIPMENT
  UF   Kitchen equipment
  NT1   Cooking appliances
    NT2   Cookers
    NT2   Microwave ovens
  RT   Catering
            Dishwashers

MICROWAVE OVENS
  BT1   Cooking appliances
    BT2   Catering equipment

J8.2. Alphabetical display accompanying systematic display

If the systematic display is to be retained as part of the published thesaurus, the accompanying alphabetical display may be in the form of an alphabetical index or an alphabetical thesaurus, modified or conventional.

(i) An alphabetical index, showing preferred and non-preferred terms, directing the user to the place for the preferred terms in the systematic display (as in Figure 35) via the notation.

Example:

CATERING EQUIPMENT   S
  UF Kitchen equipment

Kitchen equipment
  Use CATERING EQUIPMENT   S

(ii) Alphabetical thesaurus modified (with preferred place polyhierarchies). This layout (see Figure 37), found in the BSI *ROOT thesaurus* and other thesauri, may be generated by the computer, although the same result may be achieved by a manual operation. The source of the layout is the systematic display, edited as in Figure 35. The distinctive feature of this alphabetical thesaurus is that there are two sequences of broader, narrower and related terms. The first is coded plain BT/NT/RT/ and the second *BT/*NT/*RT. The asterisked entries are accompanied by the term's notation. The advantage of keeping the sequences separate and including the notation for the asterisked terms is that it distinguishes between the terms which will be displayed in the systematic schedule, following the indexing term, and those which will be found elsewhere in the display.

Figure 36. Conventional alphabetical thesaurus: catering and related fields
Derived from subject field analysis (Figure 33)

BAKERY PRODUCTS
BT   Food

BARS (licensed)
BT   Catering areas
RT   Licensing laws

BEVERAGES
UF   Drinks
RT   Food

CANTEENS
BT   Catering areas

CATERING
NT   Catering operations
RT   Catering areas
     Catering equipment
     Catering personnel
     Food
     Meals

CATERING AREAS
NT   Bars (licensed)
     Canteens
     Kitchens
     Restaurants
RT   Catering

CATERING EQUIPMENT
SN   Includes food mixers,
     cooking ware, tableware, etc.
UF   Kitchen equipment
NT   Cooking appliances
RT   Catering
     Dishwashers

CATERING MANAGEMENT
BT   Catering operations
     Management
NT   Restaruant management
RT   Catering managers
     Food purchasing

CATERING MANAGERS
BT   Catering personnel
     Managers
RT   Catering management

CATERING OPERATIONS
BT   Catering
NT   Catering management
     Food preparation
     Food purchasing
     Food service

CATERING PERSONNEL
NT   Catering managers
     Chefs
     Waiters
RT   Catering

CHEFS
UF   Cooks
BT   Catering personnel
RT   Food preparation

CONVENIENCE FOOD
UF   Fast food
BT   Food

COOKERS
BT   Cooking appliances

COOKERY
BT   Food preparation

COOKING APPLIANCES
BT   Catering equipment
     Domestic appliances
NT   Cookers
     Microwave ovens

Cooks
USE CHEFS

DAIRY PRODUCTS
BT   Food

DIET
RT   Menus

DISHWASHERS
RT   Catering equipment

DOMESTIC APPLIANCES
NT   Cooking appliances

Drinks
USE BEVERAGES

Fast food
USE CONVENIENCE FOOD

FISH
BT   Food

FOOD
NT   Bakery products
     Convenience food
     Dairy products
     Fish
     Food dishes
     Fruit
     Meat
     Vegetables
RT   Beverages
     Catering

FOOD DISHES
BT   Food
RT   Meals

FOOD PREPARATION
BT   Catering operations
NT   Cookery
RT   Chefs

FOOD PURCHASING
BT   Catering operations
     Purchasing
RT   Catering management

FOOD SERVICE
BT   Catering operations
NT   Waiting

FRUIT
BT   Food

Kitchen Equipment
USE CATERING EQUIPMENT

KITCHENS
BT   Catering areas

LICENSING LAWS
RT   Bars (licensed)

MANAGEMENT
NT   Catering management

MANAGERS
NT   Catering managers

MEALS
RT   Catering
     Food dishes
     Menus

MEAT
BT   Food

MENUS
RT   Diet
     Meals

MICROWAVE OVENS
BT   Cooking appliances

PURCHASING
NT   Food purchasing

RESTAURANT MANAGEMENT
BT   Catering management
RT   Restaurants

RESTAURANTS
BT   Catering areas
RT   Restaurant management

VEGETABLES
BT   Food

WAITERS
BT   Catering personnel
RT   Waiting

WAITING
BT   Food service
RT   Waiters

Figure 37. Alphabetical display derived from notated systematic display

From Figure 35 (selected entries only)

CATERING EQUIPMENT   S
    SN Includes food mixers, cooking ware,
        tableware, etc.
    UF Kitchen equipment
    NT Cooking appliances
    RT Catering
   *RT Dishwashers   OCD.F

CATERING MANAGEMENT   TA
    BT Catering operations
    RT Catering managers
   *BT Management   AM
   *NT Restaurant management   UMA
   *RT Food purchasing   TF

CATERING MANAGERS   TAB
    RT Catering management
   *BT Catering personnel   RB
       Managers   AMB

CATERING PERSONNEL   RB
    RT Catering
   *NT Catering managers   TAB
       Chefs   TKB
       Waiters   TPD.B

CHEFS   THB
    UF Cooks
    RT Food preparation
   *BT Catering personnel   RB

COOKING APPLIANCES   SJ
    BT Catering equipment
    NT Cookers
       Microwave ovens
   *BT Domestic appliances   OAD

DOMESTIC APPLIANCES   OAD
    RT Household technologies
   *NT Cooking appliances   SJ

FOOD PURCHASING   TF
    BT Catering operations
   *BT Purchasing   AMQ
   *RT Catering management   TA

MANAGEMENT   AM
    RT Managers
       Purchasing
   *NT Catering management   TA

MANAGERS   AMB
    RT Management
   *NT Catering managers   TAB

PURCHASING   AMQ
    RT Management
   *NT Food purchasing   TF

RESTAURANT MANAGEMENT   UMA
    RT Restaurants
   *BT Catering management

WAITERS   TPD.B
    RT Waiting
   *BT Catering personnel   RB

Example:

CATERING EQUIPMENT S   *[Preferred term and notation in systematic display]*

    SN   Includes food mixers, cooking ware, tableware, etc   *[Scope note. Information already in edited systematic display]*

    UF   Kitchen equipment   *[Quasi-synonym]*

    NT   Cooking appliances   *[NT at 1 level down in systematic display]*

    RT   Catering   *[Superordinate RT, 1 level up. Coded RT in systematic display]*

   *RT   Dishwashers   OCD.F   *[Related term in another part of the display. With notation. Information already in the edited systematic display]*

CATERING PERSONNEL   RB   *[Preferred term with notation]*

    RT   Catering   *[Superordinate RT, 1 level up Coded RT in systematic display]*

   *NT   Catering managers   TAB   *[Narrower terms in another part of the same field of the systematic display. Information already in the edited systematic display]*
                Chefs   THB
                Waiters   TPD.B

WAITERS TPD.B   *[Preferred term and notation]*

    RT   Waiting   *[Superordinate RT, 1 level up. Coded RT in systematic display]*

   *BT   Catering personnel   RB   *[Broader term in another part of the same section of the display with notation. Information already given in the edited display]*

(iii) Alphabetical thesaurus in conventional form. The thesaurus accompanying the systematic display (Figure 35) may be organized as for a conventional thesaurus. The *BT/*NTs and *RTs would be interfiled with the plain BT/NT/RTs. If required, the asterisks and accompanying notation might be omitted, although dropping the notation loses the immediate access via the notation to those broader, narrower and related terms separated in the systematic display from the preferred term under which they are entered in the alphabetical thesaurus.

J9. Final checking with experts

The compilers should have been in contact with subject specialists during all stages of construction (J5.4) and should not finalize and produce the thesaurus before it is approved and accepted by these experts. Relevant sections of the thesaurus should be discussed personally with one or two experts in the appropriate subject fields.

J10. Introduction to the thesaurus

The thesaurus is not complete until a comprehensive introduction has been written covering most, if not all, of the following points:

○ The purpose of the thesaurus.

○ The subject coverage, with an indication of which are the core and peripheral fields.

○ The total number of indexing terms used, with a breakdown showing the number of preferred and non-preferred terms.

○ Vocabulary control: the standards used and the rules adopted regarding choice and form of indexing terms.

○ Structure and interrelationships: the standards used and the rules adopted.

○ Thesaurus layout and displays: explanation of the function of the individual displays.

○ The filing rules used, with reference to the standards used, if any.

○ The meanings of all conventions and abbreviations and punctuation marks used in a non-standardized form should be clarified.

○ Operational use of the thesaurus: guidance on use in different types of systems – pre-coordinate, post-coordinate, manual and computerized.

○ Updating and maintenance: details of updating policy and the name and address of the agency responsible for maintaining the thesaurus.

○ Acknowledgement of written sources used.

○ Personal acknowledgements: addressed to subject experts and others who may have assisted with the compilation.

These points should be well illustrated by examples, wherever possible.

J11. Editing

○ Check reciprocal entries: the use of a computer relieves the compiler of much of this work (see Section L).

○ Check the notation in the systematic display – looking especially for confusion between the letter s and the number 5, and between the letters s and z, u and v.

○ Check the form of terms, spelling, etc.: pay special attention to consistency in the use of hyphens.

○ Check the alphabetization: again this is not a problem in computer-produced thesauri.

○ In the systematic section check the indenting, spacing and layout. Pay particular attention to the indenting, because if it is incorrect, the BT/NT/RT relations derived from it in the alphabetical thesaurus will be at best misleading and at worst nonsensical.

○ Decide on the typeface, size, and style to be used in graphic and systematic displays (J7.3) and also in the alphabetical display. Decide also on the layout for the alphabetical display. For example, is it to be in a two or three column arrangement? If the latter this may mean changes in page and type size.

J12. Testing

Use the thesaurus to index a selection of documents. At least 500–1,000 documents should be indexed before the language is finalized. This may be done by using a semi-published draft of the thesaurus. Test the thesaurus against queries that have been put to the system as well as by document indexing. These exercises are likely to reveal gaps in coverage and will lead to the addition of new terms and an extension of the entry vocabulary, as well as to changes of emphasis in the relationship between the terms.

In some situations the new thesaurus may be used alongside the old system over a period of time to index new accessions. Maintaining this dual system makes heavy demands on the staff but has been reported to be worthwhile (62).

J13. Production for publication

A draft thesaurus should be prepared for discussion and testing before final publication. If computer-produced, the draft thesaurus may be in the form of a computer print-out (rather bulky for a large thesaurus) or on microfiche. When the draft is tested and corrected, the amended version may be made available for online display and for photocomposition and printing.

Thesaurus printing for publication is not covered in this manual. The production method chosen will depend on whether the thesaurus is computer-compiled, the size of the publication, the number of copies required, and other factors, such as whether the thesaurus is for limited internal use or for sale to the general public.

J14. Deposit with clearing house

A copy of the thesaurus and subsequent editions should be deposited at Aslib in the United Kingdom, and at the appropriate national centre in other countries, and also with the relevant international clearing house:

For thesauri in the English language, including multilingual thesauri containing English-language sections:

> Thesaurus Clearinghouse
> The Library
> Faculty of Library Science
> University of Toronto
> 140 St George Street
> Toronto
> Ontario M5S 1A1
> Canada

For thesauri in other languages:

> Instytut Informacji Naukowej, Technicznej i Ekonomicznej (IINTE)
> Zurawia 3/5
> 00-926 Warsaw
> Poland

Section K

Thesaurus maintenance and updating

An indexing language is out of date as soon as, if not before, it is published, so that any 'live' thesaurus must be updated regularly. Thesauri with specific vocabularies applied in systems using depth indexing tend to require updating more frequently than those confined to the use of more static, broader concepts. As would be expected, the need for modification increases, whatever the nature of the vocabulary or depth of indexing, as the number of documents that are indexed increases. The thesaurus grows most rapidly in the early stages of database development and levels off subsequently. At a later date, a further burst of growth may occur if the subject coverage of the database is extended.

K1. Thesaurus modifications

Changes to be made fall into three categories: adding new concepts and deleting or amending existing terms.

K1.1. Addition of new concepts
New preferred terms are added for concepts arising in indexing and searching. These are usually but not always central to the subject field. New terms should be inserted with all relevant scope notes, synonyms, hierarchies and associative relationships. Concepts too specific for the depth required or marginal to the subject field may be treated as non-preferred terms, giving access to the nearest broader term or to two or more terms used in combination.

K1.2. Deletion of terms
Terms which are misleading, incorrect or rarely used are deleted together with all their relationships. Some deleted terms may be retained in the thesaurus, but as non-preferred terms leading to the nearest broader preferred terms.

K1.3. Amendments to existing term entries
Amendments may include simple changes, such as spelling corrections, or changes from the singular to the plural form. More intricate amendments consist of addition or modification of scope notes, and additions and deletions of synonyms and other relationships. Other complex amendments arise when the classes in systematic thesauri or the tables in graphic displays require reorganization.

K2. Maintenance and updating routines

Thesaurus updating needs to be managed methodically, otherwise confusion results in indexing and searching. In tasks of maintenance and updating, the computer is an invaluable aid, relieving the tedium of clerical operations, ensuring accuracy and providing speedy communication of changes to the users of the system (see Section L). The control of thesaurus updating is usually in the hands of one compiler or a team of compilers. Candidate terms, proposed by indexers or searchers, are scrutinized by the thesaurus editors, with the aid of experts, where necessary. Those terms which are accepted are added to the thesaurus with the necessary scope notes and relationships, and in the correct place in the alphabetical, systematic and graphical sequences. The thesaurus editors also decide on term deletion and amendments to existing terms. In machine-held thesauri, the clerical tasks of adding or removing inter-term relationships and correcting the form of amended terms, wherever they may occur in the thesaurus, is carried out automatically. A record should be kept of thesaurus changes, in the form of term histories, noting additions, deletions and amendments, with accompanying dates. In some computerized systems, search terms are automatically mapped on to the corrected terms, using the information supplied by the term histories.

It is essential that users should be aware of changes with minimum delay. In manual systems, especially when the thesaurus is used by a number of different information systems, alerting users to thesaurus changes is a difficult problem. With thesauri compiled and updated by computer the task of communication is simplified. If the thesaurus is viewed online, amendments are immediately seen by users. Another advantage is that hard-copy editions of the thesaurus may be produced annually or bi-annually from the thesaurus database without the editorial and typing costs required for the same operations performed manually. Computer-produced printed lists of amendments may also be provided more economically than by manual systems.

Computer aids

In a human-compiled thesaurus the computer is used to perform routine operations which are error-prone and time-consuming when undertaken manually. The computer is also important as the agent which generates the printed thesaurus, makes it available online for consultation, and holds it as the master vocabulary file in an information retrieval system. In a thesaurus which is not compiled by human intellectual effort but is automatically generated, the computer is used to handle the statistical and linguistic data involved in determining term relationships. (See F6.)

Among the tasks performed by computers to aid the intellectual processes of the human compiler are selecting terms, recording preliminary details and handling thesaurus structure.

L1. Selection of terms and recording of preliminary details

The computer may be used to record details of terms manually selected from standardized sources and from literature and questions scanning. (See J5.2.1 and J6.) If frequency data is included, print-out of the terms in order of frequency of occurrence as well as lists in alphabetical and broad class order may be produced. Inverted entries for compound terms, which may also be produced, give a rough subject grouping. The computer may also be used to select terms automatically from the documents. (See J5.2.2.)

L2. Handling thesaurus structure

The intellectual process of 'finding structure' (see J7) is carried out by the human compiler, but when the structure is found it may be manipulated, maintained and updated by the computer.

L2.1. Automatic generation of reciprocals
The computer generates reciprocal entries for the basic thesaural relationships:

Example:

ALCOHOLIC BEVERAGES
    UF Alcoholic drinks
    BT Beverages
    NT Beer
          Cider
          Spirits
          Wine
    RT Alcoholism

Automatically generated reciprocals:

Alcoholic drinks USE ALCOHOLIC BEVERAGES

BEVERAGES	NT	Alcoholic beverages
BEER	BT	Alcoholic beverages
CIDER	BT	Alcoholic beverages
SPIRITS	BT	Alcoholic beverages
WINE	BT	Alcoholic beverages
ALCOHOLISM	RT	Alcoholic beverages

L2.2. Generating additional displays

The structure may be expanded in the following ways:

From the alphabetical display:
Permuted index (see H1.3)
Machine-generated hierarchies (see H2)

From the systematic display:
Alphabetical display (see H3.3 and J7.3, J8.2)

From the graphic display:
Alphabetical display (see H4)

L2.3. Production of printed thesaurus

With the aid of the computer the thesaurus, or part of the thesaurus, may be printed in hard copy, whether as computer print-out, or after photocomposition, in a form having good typographic quality, suitable for publishing. Alternatively, microform copies may be produced using COM facilities.

L2.4. Thesaurus maintenance: deletions, additions and amendments

The computer implements changes in the thesaurus arising out of the day-to-day operation of the thesaurus (see Section K). The intellectual decisions are made by the compilers and indexers. The computer carries out the necessary clerical tasks. The computer program ensures that the new terms are added in the correct alphabetical sequence and that all reciprocals are made. When a term is deleted, all reciprocal links are removed automatically. If the form of a term is altered, or a narrower term substituted for a related term, the computer program ensures that the corrections will be implemented in all reciprocal entries.

L3. The thesaurus in operational situations: use in indexing and searching

With computer aids, the thesaurus can play an important role in the operation of an information storage and retrieval system serving as the master vocabulary file.

L3.1. Master vocabulary file

This master file is used to check the indexing terms used by indexers and searchers. Unacceptable terms are rejected, and in some systems, if non-preferred terms are entered, the preferred terms are automatically substituted. If indexing policy requires, the software may provide automatic posting onto selected generic terms for each preferred term used in indexing. Other tasks performed by the master file include the generation of 'see' and 'see also' references for printed indexes, recording details of frequency of posting of preferred terms, and recording and updating the history of indexing term changes. In some systems, discontinued terms are automatically switched to current terms when used by indexers or searchers.

L3.2. Thesaurus display online

The thesaurus may be made available for viewing online. The ease with which this is achieved varies according to the quality of the software available. On entering the required term, it is standard practice to scan the terms in the immediate vicinity of the required term in the alphabetical sequence, and to expand the detail under any particular term either fully, or in part. It is also possible to scan the appropriate sections of hierarchical and systematic displays. Terms are usually selected from the display by quoting identifying codes. Not only single terms and their immediate relationships but whole hierarchies or categories of systematic displays may, in some systems, be selected and incorporated into search strategies.

L4. Merging of thesauri

Computer aids permit the merging of machine-readable thesauri.

Section M   *Packages and bureau services*

This is a rapidly developing field and this section is likely to become out of date relatively quickly. Readers are advised to check with the Aslib Information Resources Centre.

ADLIB

Developed and marketed by:
Databasix Ltd
Strawberry Hill House
Old Bath Road
Newbury
Berks. RG13 1NG
United Kingdom
Tel. (0635) 37373

Thesaurus management facility is part of the total package. Also offers a bureau service for thesaurus production.

ASSASSIN 6

Developed and marketed by:
Imperial Chemical Industries plc
Agricultural Division
Associated Knowledge Systems
Daryl House
Bridge Road
Stockton-on-Tees
Cleveland TS28 3BW
United Kingdom
Tel. (0642) 677296

Thesaurus management facility is an integral part of the text retrieval package. Wide range of features including own choice of relationships, control of synonyms and systonyms (undifferentiated synonyms), automatic post up.

ASTUTE

Developed by:
Commission of the European Communities
Directorate General for Scientific and Technical Information and Information Management
DG XIII-B
Bâtiment Jean Monnet
Plateau Kirchberg
Luxembourg L–2920
Tel. (352) 2920

Bureau services extend to the Commission only. Handles multilingual thesauri up to five languages.

BASIS

> *Developed by:*
> Battelle Columbus Laboratory
> BASIS Coordinator
> 505 King Avenue
> Columbus, OH43201
> USA
> Tel. (614) 4244062
>
> *UK contact:*
> Battelle Institute Ltd
> BASIS Coordinator
> 15 Hanover Square
> London W1R 9AJ
> United Kingdom
> Tel. (01) 493 0184

Thesaurus management facility is part of the BASIS data management and retrieval system. Special features: multilingual capacity, automatic posting up to selected terms during indexing.

BIBLIOTECH LIBRARY SYSTEM
Biblio-techniques Library and Information System (BLIS)

> *Developed by:*
> Advanced Data Management Inc.
> c/o Comstow Information Services
> 302 Boxboro Road
> Stow, MA 01775
> USA
> Tel. (617) 897 7163

Online library management system (including online catalogues). The thesaurus management module is part of the package.

CAIRS and MICROCAIRS

> *Developed and marketed by:*
> Leatherhead Food RA
> Randalls Road
> Leatherhead
> Surrey KT22 7RY
> United Kingdom
> Tel. (0372) 376761
>
> *Microcairs is also marketed by:*
> RTZ Computer Services Ltd
> 1 Redcliff Street
> Bristol BS99 7JS
> United Kingdom
> Tel. (0272) 24181

Thesaurus management software is part of the CAIRS package.

CALM

Developed and marketed by:
Pyramid Software Products
9 Church Street
Reading
Berks. RG1 2SB
United Kingdom
Tel. (0734) 595633

Thesaurus management software called THESAURUS is part of a library management package, but may be purchased separately. Operates on microcomputers.

COMPUTERCRAFT

Developed by Robin Bonner for:
The Bliss Classification Association
Honorary Secretary
Chris Preddle
c/o Library and Resource Centre
Commonwealth Institute
Kensington High Street
London W8 6NG
United Kingdom
or
ASSIA
Library Association Publishing Ltd
7 Ridgmount Street
London WC1E 7AE.
United Kingdom
Tel. (01) 580 1848

in co-operation with
Computercraft
272–276 Pentonville Road
London N1 9JY
United Kingdom
Tel. (01) 833 0143

Software for the production of classification schedules, with the facility for derivation of a near-*ROOT* style alphabetical thesaurus from the classified schedules. May be run on microcomputers.

CORMORANT

Developed and marketed by:
Kent-Barlow Publications Ltd
Kingsmead House
250 Kings Road
Chelsea
London SW3 5UE
United Kingdom
Tel. (01) 351 2776

Window technique allowing thesaurus display to support controlled indexing.

GRIPS/DIRS

> *Developed and marketed by:*
> Deutsches Institut für Medizinische Dokumentation
>   und Information (DIMDI)
> Weisshausstr. 27
> Postfach 420580
> D-5000 Köln 41
> Federal Republic of Germany
> Tel. (0221) 47241
>
> Thesaurus management facility is part of the information retrieval software. Can handle tree structures in explosion–type searches.

INQUIRE

> *Developed by:*
> Infodata Systems Inc.
> 5205 Leesburg Pike
> Falls Church, VA 22041
> USA
> Tel. (703) 578 3430
>
> *UK contact:*
> Thorn EMI Computer Software
> Ringwood House
> Walton Street
> Aylesbury
> Bucks. HP21 7OL
> United Kingdom
> Tel. (0296) 32011
>
> Thesaurus management facility is part of the data management system.

MINISIS

> *Developed by:*
> International Development Research Centre
> Information Sciences Division
> PO Box 8500
> 60 Queen Street
> Ottawa, ON
> Canada K1G 3H9
> Tel. (613) 236 6163
>
> *UK agent:*
> Assyst (UK)
> Computer Services Ltd
> Arden House
> West Street
> Leighton Buzzard
> Beds. LU7 7DD
> United Kingdom
> Tel. (0525) 382626
>
> Thesaurus management software. Multilingual capability (up to ten languages).

POLYDOC

> *Developed by:*
> Norwegian Centre for Informatics
> Postboks 350
> Blindern
> 0314 Oslo 3
> Norway
> Tel. (2) 452010
>
> *UK contact:*
> Alistair Crawford
> Intercom Data Systems Ltd
> Woodsted House
> 72 Chertsey Road
> Woking
> Surrey GU21 5BJ
> United Kingdom
> Tel. (04862) 26951
>
> The thesaurus management system will be part of a small library system package.

PYRAMID

> *See* CALM

QDMS

> *Marketed by:*
> Comset Ltd
> International Marketing
> 8 Hanechoshet Street
> Tel-Aviv 61131
> Israel
> Tel. (03) 482736
>
> The thesaurus management facility is part of the data management system. Handles multilingual thesauri.

RASMUS

> *Developed and marketed by:*
> Cambridge Software Ltd
> PO Box 3
> Ely
> Cambs. CB7 4AX
> United Kingdom
> Tel. (0353) 4444
>
> The thesaurus management software is part of the bibliographic database system.

ROOT

Developed for:
British Standards Institution
Information Department
Linford Wood
Milton Keynes
Bucks. MK14 6LE
United Kingdom
Tel. (0908) 320066

Marketed by:
Hutton & Rostron Data Processing Ltd
Netley House
Gomshall
Surrey GU5 9QA
United Kingdom
Tel. (048) 641 3221

Thesaurus management system. Bureau services only. Special features. Alphabetical display derived from systematic display. Multilingual capability.

STRIDE, MICRO STRIDE

Developed by:
BNF Metals Technology Centre
Grove Laboratories
Denchworth Road
Wantage
Oxon OX12 9BJ
United Kingdom
Tel. (02357) 2992

Thesaurus management system. (Creation, maintenance, and use with STATUS systems as master vocabulary file.) Wide range of online and hard-copy displays may be generated. May be used independently of STATUS.

TINTERM

Developed by:
IME – Information Management & Engineering Ltd
1 Carthusian Street
London EC1M 6EB
United Kingdom
Tel. (01) 253 1177

The thesaurus management software is an integral part of the TINMAN system (a microcomputer system based on the entity-relation model).

TITUS

Developed by:
Institut Français du Textile
35 rue des Abondances
92100 Boulogne-sur-Seine
France
Tel. (21) 825 1890

The thesaurus management software is part of the information storage and retrieval system. Multilingual capacity up to four languages.

UNIDAS

Developed by:
Sperry Ltd
PO Box 1100
6231 Sulzbach/TS
Federal Republic of Germany
Tel. (49) 6197001

Available from:
Scicon Computer Services Ltd
Brick Close
Kiln Farm
Milton Keynes MK11 3EJ
United Kingdom
Tel: (0908) 565656

The thesaurus management facility is part of the document retrieval system. Has multilingual capability.

Bibliography

General

1. Aitchison, Jean. Bliss and the thesaurus: the Bibliographic Classification of H. E. Bliss as a source of thesaurus terms and structure. Paper submitted to the International Conference on Ranganathan's Philosophy. New Delhi, India: November 1985. Subsequently published as: A classification as a source for a thesaurus: the Bibliographic Classification of H. E. Bliss as a source of thesaurus terms and structure. *Journal of Documentation*, vol. 42, no. 3, September 1986, pp. 160–181

2. Aitchison, Jean. Indexing languages: classification schemes and thesauri. In: *Handbook of special librarianship and information work*, Anthony, L.J. (ed.), 5th ed. London: Aslib, 1982. Chapter 10, pp. 207–261

3. Aitchison, Jean. 'Integrated thesaurus of the social sciences: design study', prepared for UNESCO Division for the International Development of the Social Sciences. Paris: UNESCO, 1981. Private publication

4. Aitchison, Jean. Integration of thesauri in the social sciences. *International Classification*, vol. 8, no. 2, 1981, pp. 75–85

5. Aitchison, T. M., and Harding, P. Automatic indexing and classification for mechanised information retrieval. *Information management research in Europe. Proceedings of the EURIM 5 Conference, Versailles, France, May 1982.* London: Aslib, 1983, pp. 47–55

6. American National Standards Institute. ANSI Z39.19: *Guidelines for thesaurus structure, construction and use.* New York: ANSI, 1980

7. *Aslib Information* (monthly). London: Aslib, 1973 to date

8. Aslib Library. *Bibliography of mono- and multilingual vocabularies, thesauri, subject headings and classification schemes in the social sciences*, prepared in collaboration with Jean Aitchison and C. G. Allen. Paris: UNESCO, 1982. (Reports and papers in the social sciences, no. 54)

9. Association Française de Normalisation. *Règles d'établissement des thesaurus en langue française.* NFZ 47–100. Paris: AFNOR, 1974

10. Austin, D. The CRG research into a freely faceted scheme. In: Maltby, A. (ed.) *Classification in the 1980s: a second look.* London: Clive Bingley, 1976, pp. 158–159

11. Austin, D. *PRECIS: a manual of concept analysis and subject indexing*, 2nd ed. London: British Library, 1984

12. Baumgartner, R. *Problems and opportunities in thesaurus development for numeric databases. In: Proceedings of the 45th ASIS Annual Meeting*, vol. 19, 1982, pp. 26–28. (Predicast thesauri)

13. Bhattacharyya, G. Classaurus: its fundamentals, design and use. In: Dahlberg, I. (ed.). *Universal classification I: subject analysis and ordering systems*. Proceedings of the 4th International Study Conference on Classification Research, FID/CR, Augsburg, 28 June – 2 July 1982. Frankfurt: INDEKS Verlag, 1982, pp. 139–148

14. British Standards Institution. BS 5723: *Guidelines for the establishment and development of monolingual thesauri*, 2nd ed. London: BSI, 1987

15. British Standards Institution. BS 6723: *Guidelines for the establishment and development of multilingual thesauri.* London: BSI, 1985

16. Buchanan, Brian. *Theory of library classification.* London: Clive Bingley, 1979. Chapters 5 and 6, Construction of a faceted scheme

17. Cleverdon, C. W., Keen, M., and Mills, J. *Factors determining the performance of indexing systems: an investigation supported by a grant to Aslib by the National Science Foundation.* Cranfield, England: Aslib Cranfield Research Project, 1966

18. Crafts-Lighty, A., and others. The use of ADLIB and the ROOT thesaurus to manage a special library. In: *7th International Online Information Meeting, London, 6–8 December 1983.* Oxford: Learned Information, 1983, pp. 465–469

19. Croft, W. B. Experiments with representation in a document retrieval system. *Information Technology Research and Development* (GB), vol. 2, no. 1, January 1983, pp. 1–21

20. Croghan, A. *A manual on the construction of an indexing language using educational technology as an example.* London: Carburgh Publications, 1971

21. *Current Awareness Bulletin* (monthly). London: Aslib, 1984 to date

22. Dahlberg, I. Classification literature: 04. Classification systems and thesauri. In: *International Classification* (monthly). Frankfurt: INDEKS Verlag

23. Dahlberg, I. *Ontical structures and universal classification.* Bangalore, India: Sarada Ranganathan Endowment for Library Science, 1978, p. 42, The Systematifier

24. Deutsches Institut für Normung (DIN). *Richtlinien für die Herstellung und Weiterentwicklung von Thesauri.* DIN 1463 – 1976. Berlin: DIN, 1976

25. Dextre, S. G., and Clarke, T. M. A system for machine-aided thesaurus construction. *Aslib Proceedings*, vol. 33, no. 3, March 1981, pp. 102–112

26. Doszkocs, T. E. AID, an Associated Interactive Dictionary for online searching. *Online Review*, vol. 2, no. 2, June 1978, pp. 163–173

27. Doszkocs, T. E., and Rapp, B. A. Searching MEDLINE in English: a prototype user interface with natural language query, ranked output, and relevance feedback. *Proceedings of the ASIS Annual Meeting*, vol. 16, 1979, pp. 131-139

28. Dubois, C. P. R. The use of thesauri in online retrieval. *Journal of Information Science Principles & Practice* (Netherlands), vol. 8, no. 2, March 1984, pp. 63–66

29. Fédération International de Documentation (FID). *Classification systems and thesauri 1950–1982.* (Vol. 1 of *International Classification and Indexing Bibliography*, ICIB 1). Frankfurt: INDEKS Verlag, 1982. (FID – Publ. 610)

30. Foskett, A. C. *Subject approach to information*, 4th ed. London: Bingley, 1982

31. Foskett, D. J. *The construction of a faceted classification for a special subject.* London: Butterworth, 1959

32. Foskett, D. J. Thesaurus. In: *Encyclopaedia of library and information science*, vol. 30. New York: Marcel Dekker, Inc., 1981

33. Fugmann, Robert. The complementarity of natural and indexing languages. In: Perreault, J. M., and Dahlberg, I. (eds). *Universal classification II: subject analysis and ordering systems.* Proceedings of the 4th International Study Conference on Classification Research, FID/CR, Augsburg, 28 June – 2 July 1982. Frankfurt: INDEKS Verlag, 1982/83, pp. 86–89

34. Gesellschaft für Information und Dokumentation (GID). *Thesaurus guide. Analytical directory of selected vocabularies for information retrieval.* Prepared for the Commission of the European Communities by GID. Amsterdam: North Holland, 1985

35. Gilbert, Valerie. A list of thesauri and subject heading lists held in the Aslib Library. *Aslib Proceedings,* vol. 31, no. 6, June 1979, pp. 264–271

36. Gilchrist, Alan. *The thesaurus in retrieval.* London: Aslib, 1971

37. Hack, John. Search aids for American Petroleum Institute databases. *Database,* vol. 7, no. 4, December 1984, pp. 84–88

38. Horsnell, V. The Intermediate Lexicon: an aid to international cooperation. *Aslib Proceedings,* vol. 27, no. 2, February 1975, pp. 57–66

39. Horsnell, V. *Intermediate lexicon for information science: a feasibility study.* London: Polytechnic of North London, School of Librarianship, 1974

40. Horsnell, V., and Merrett, A. *Intermediate lexicon research project: Phase 2. Evaluation of the switching and retrieval performance of the intermediate lexicon for information science.* London: Polytechnic of North London, School of Librarianship, 1978

41. Institute for Scientific, Technical and Economic Information (IINTE). *Bibliographic Bulletin of the Clearinghouse at IINTE.* Annual list of the holdings of the clearinghouse for thesauri, descriptor, keyword and subject heading lists, classification systems and schedules in languages other than English. With supplements. Warsaw: The Institute, 1970 to date

42. International Organization for Standardization. ISO 2788: *Guidelines for the establishment and development of monolingual thesauri,* 2nd ed. Geneva: ISO, 1986

43. International Organization for Standardization. ISO 5964: *Guidelines for the establishment and development of multilingual thesauri.* Geneva: ISO, 1985

44. Johnston, S. M. Effect of thesaurus indexing on retrieval from machine-readable databases. *Quarterly Bulletin of IAALD,* vol. 27, no. 3, 1982, pp. 90–96

45. Knapp, S. D. Creating BRS/TERM, a vocabulary database for searchers. *DATABASE,* vol. 7, no. 4, December 1984, pp. 70–75

46. Lancaster, F. W. *Vocabulary control for information retrieval,* 2nd ed. Arlington, Virginia: Information Resources Press, 1986

47. MaCafferty, Maxine. *Thesauri and thesaurus construction.* London: Aslib, 1977

48. Markey, Karen, and Atherton, P. *ONTAP: Online training and practice manual for ERIC data base searchers.* Syracuse: Syracuse University, ERIC Clearinghouse on Information Resources, 1978

49. Markey, Karen, and others. An analysis of controlled vocabulary and free text search statements in online searches. *Online Review*, vol. 4, no. 3, 1979, pp. 225–236

50. Niehoff, R. T., and Kwasny, S. The role of automated subject switching in a distributed information network. *Online Review*, vol. 3, no. 2, June 1979, pp. 181–194

51. Niehoff, R. T., and Mack, G. *Final report on evaluation of the Vocabulary Switching System.* NSF Grant IST-7911190 and IST-8111497 for National Science Foundation. Division of Information Science and Technology. Columbus, Ohio: Battelle Columbus Laboratories, 1984. Summary in: *International Classification*, vol. 12, no. 1, 1985, pp. 2–6

52. Niehoff, R. T., and Mack, G. The Vocabulary Switching System: description of evaluation studies. *International Classification*, vol. 12, no. 1, 1985, pp. 2–6

53. Niehoff, R. T., and others. *The design and evaluation of a Vocabulary Switching System for use in multi-base search environments.* Columbus: Battelle Columbus Laboratories, 1980

54. *Online Notes* (monthly). London: Aslib, 1979 to date

55. Orna, Elizabeth. *Build yourself a thesaurus: a step by step guide.* Norwich: Running Angel, 1983

56. Perez, Ernest. Text enhancement. Controlled vocabulary vs free text. *Special Libraries*, vol. 73, no. 3, July 1982, pp. 183–192

57. Piternick, Anne B. Searching vocabularies: a developing vocabulary of online search tools. *Online Review*, vol. 8, no. 5, 1984, pp. 441–449

58. Ranganathan, S. R. *The Colon Classification.* Rutgers, The State University, Graduate School of Library Science, 1965. (Rutgers series on systems for the intellectual organization of knowledge, by Susan Artandi, vol. 4)

59. Rolling, L. Computer management of multilingual thesauri. *Aslib Proceedings*, vol. 23, no. 11, November 1971, pp. 591–594

60. Salton, G., and McGill, M. J. *Introduction to modern information retrieval.* New York: McGraw Hill, 1983

61. Sievert, Mary Ellen, and Boyce, Bert R. Hedge trimming and the resurrection of the controlled vocabulary on line. *Online Review*, vol. 7, no. 6, 1983, pp. 489–494

62. Smith, Inese A. Development of indexing systems at the National Youth Bureau. *Catalogue and Index*, no. 74, Summer 1984, pp. 1–4

63. Snow, Bonnie. Why use a database thesaurus? *Online*, vol. 9, no. 6, November 1985, pp. 92–96

64. Soergel, Dagobert. *Indexing languages and thesauri: construction and maintenance.* Los Angeles, California: Melville Publishing Co., 1974

65. Sparck Jones, K. Automatic classification. In: Maltby, A. *Classification in the 70s: a second look.* London: Clive Bingley, 1976, pp. 209–225

66. Sparck Jones, K. *Automatic indexing, 1974: a state-of-the-art review.* Cambridge: University of Cambridge, 1974

67. Stevens, M. E. *Automatic indexing: a state-of-the-art review.* Washington, D.C.: National Bureau of Standards, 1980

68. Townley, H. M., and Gee, R. D. *Thesaurus-making: grow your own word-stock.* London: Andre Deutsch, 1980

69. Vickery, B. C. *Faceted classification: a guide to construction and use of special schemes.* London: Aslib, 1960

Thesauri and classification systems

70. Aitchison, Jean. 'ECOT thesaurus: educational courses and occupations thesaurus', prepared for ECCTIS and the Department of Education and Science, working edition. Milton Keynes, England: Open University, ECCTIS, 1984

71. Aitchison, Jean. *UNESCO thesaurus: a structured list of descriptors for indexing and retrieving literature in the fields of education, science, and social sciences, culture and communication.* Paris: UNESCO, 1977. 2 vols

72. Aitchison, Jean, Brewin, Paul, and Cotton, Joanna. *DHSS-DATA thesaurus.* London: Department of Health and Social Security, 1985

73. Aitchison, Jean, Gomersall, A., and Ireland, R. *Thesaurofacet: a thesaurus and faceted classification for engineering and related subjects.* Whetstone, Leicester, England: English Electric Company Ltd, 1969

74. Aitchison, Jean, and others. *Thesaurus on youth: an integrated classification and thesaurus on youth affairs and related topics.* Compiled in association with Inese A. Smith and Susan Thompson. Leicester, England: National Youth Bureau, 1981

75. American Petroleum Institute. *API thesaurus*, 21st ed. Washington, DC: API, 1984

76. 'Art and architecture thesaurus'. North Bennington, Vt: The Getty Art History Information Programme. (in progress)

77. Askew, Colin. *Thesaurus of consumer terms*. London: The Consumers Association; The Hague: International Organization of Consumers Unions, 1979–1982. 2 vols

78. Beck, Carl, and others. *Political science thesaurus II*, 2nd ed., revised. Pittsburgh: American Political Science Association, University Center for International Studies, University of Pittsburgh, 1979

79. Black, W. T. *Thesaurus of terms on copper technology*, 7th ed. New York: Copper Development Association, 1981

80. Bonner, Robin, and others. 'Community information classification'. London: National Association of Citizens Advice Bureaux. To be published

81. British Standards Institution. *ROOT thesaurus*, 2nd ed. Milton Keynes, England: BSI, 1985. 2 vols

82. *BSO: Broad System of Ordering: schedule and index, third revision*, prepared by the FID/BSO Panel (Eric Coates, Geoffrey Lloyd, Susan Simandi). The Hague/Paris: FID, 1978 (FID Publication no. 564)

83. *CAB thesaurus*, compiled by G. Eric Tidbury. Slough, England: Commonwealth Agricultural Bureaux, 1982. 4 vols

84. Coates, E. J. *The British catalogue of music classification*. London: British National Bibliography, 1960

85. Commission of the European Communities. *Food: multilingual thesaurus*, 2nd English ed. London: Clive Bingley, K. G. Saur, 1979

86. *Construction industry thesaurus*, 2nd ed., compiled by the CIT at the Polytechnic of the South Bank under the direction of Michael J. Roberts. London: Department of the Environment, Property Services Agency, 1976

87. Defriez, Philip. *The ISDD thesaurus. Keywords relating to the non-medical use of drugs and drug dependence*. London: Institute for the Study of Drug Dependence, 1980

88. *EURATOM thesaurus*, 2nd ed. Brussels: European Atomic Energy Community, 1966–70. 2 vols

89. *INSPEC thesaurus*. London: Institution of Electrical Engineers. (biennial)

90. International Bureau of Education. *UNESCO: IBE education thesaurus: a list of terms for indexing and retrieving documents and data in the field of education, with French and Spanish equivalents*, 4th revised ed. Paris: UNESCO, 1984

91. International Labour Office. *ILO thesaurus*, 3rd ed. Geneva: the Office, 1985. 2 vols

92. *International Road Research Documentation (IRRD) thesaurus*, 2nd edition. Paris: OECD, 1985. 2 vols

93. *International technical thesaurus. Noriane/Isonet databases on standards*, English version. Paris: AFNOR, 1981. 2 vols

94. Manpower Services Commission. *Classification of occupations and directory of occupational titles (CODOT)*. London: HMSO, 1972–82, 3 vols, supplement

95. *Medical Subject Headings (MeSH)*. Bethesda, MD: National Library of Medicine. Annual update

96. *Metallurgical thesaurus*. Luxembourg: Système de Documentation et d'Information Metallurgique des Communautés Européenes (SDIM), 1975

97. Mills, J., and Broughton, V. *Bliss Bibliographic Classification*, 2nd ed. *Introduction and auxiliary schedules; Class H Anthropology, Human Biology, Health Sciences; Class I Psychology and Psychiatry; Class J Education; Class K Society; Class P Religion; Class Q Social Welfare; Class T Economics and Enterprise Management*. Penultimate schedules: 'Class C Chemistry; Class E/G Biological Science; Class R Political Science and Politics'. London: Butterworth, 1977–. In progress

98. Pharmaceutical Society of Great Britain. *Martindale online: drug information thesaurus and user's guide*, prepared by the Martindale staff in the Department of Pharmaceutical Sciences. London: Pharmaceutical Press, 1984

99. *SPINES thesaurus, a controlled and structured vocabulary of science and technology for policy making, management and development*. Paris: UNESCO, 1976

100. *TDCK circular thesaurus system*. The Hague: Netherlands Armed Forces Technical Documentation and Information Centre, 1963

101. *Thesaurus of engineering and scientific terms (TEST): a list of scientific and engineering terms and their relationships for use as a vocabulary in indexing and retrieving technical information*. New York: Engineers Joint Council and US Department of Defense, 1967

102. *Thesaurus of ERIC descriptors*, by Lyn Barnett, Jim Houston and Pat Coulter, 9th ed. Prepared for the US Department of Education. Phoenix, Arizona: Oryx, 1982

103. *UNBIS thesaurus: list of terms used in indexing and cataloging of documents and other materials relevant to United Nations programmes and activities*. New York: United Nations Bibliographic Information Systems, 1981

104. Viet, Jean. *EUDISED multilingual thesaurus for information processing in the field of education*, English version. Paris: Mouton; Strasbourg: Council of Europe, 1973

105. Viet, Jean. *International thesaurus of cultural development*. Paris: UNESCO, 1980

106. Viet, Jean. *Macrothesaurus for information processing in the field of economic and social development*, 3rd ed. New York: United Nations, 1985

107. Viet, Jean. *Thesaurus for information processing in sociology*. The Hague: Mouton, 1971

108. Viet, Jean. *Thesaurus – mass communication*, 2nd ed. Paris: UNESCO, 1982

109. Viet, Jean, and Van Slype, G. *EUDISED multilingual thesaurus for information processing in the field of education*, English version, new ed. Berlin/New York/Amsterdam: Council of Europe, Commission of the European Communities and Mouton & Co., 1984

Acknowledgements

Figure 4: from the *Engineers Joint Council system of roles*, Battelle Memorial Institute, n.d. Reproduced by permission of the publisher.

Figure 5: from Maron, M.E., and others, *Probabilistic indexing: a statistical technique for document identification and retrieval*, TRW, 1959. Reproduced by permission of the publisher.

Figure 6: from the *Thesaurus of engineering and scientific terms*, Engineers Joint Council and US Department of Defense, 1967.

Figure 7: from Tidbury, G. Eric (Comp.), *CAB thesaurus*, Commonwealth Agricultural Bureaux, 1982. Reproduced by permission of CAB International (formerly the Commonwealth Agricultural Bureaux).

Figure 8: from Beck, C., and others, *Political science thesaurus II*, 2nd ed., revised, University Center for International Studies, University of Pittsburgh/American Political Science Association, 1979.

Figure 9: from the *INSPEC thesaurus*, INSPEC, 1987. Reproduced by permission from INSPEC.

Figures 10 and 12: reprinted from the *Thesaurus of ERIC descriptors*, with permission from The Oryx Press, 2214 North Central Ave., Phoenix, AZ 85004, USA.

Figure 11: from *Medical Subject Headings*. National Library of Medicine, 1986. Reproduced by permission of the publisher.

Figure 13: from the *UNESCO: IBE education thesaurus*, 4th revised ed., UNESCO, 1984. Reproduced by permission of the publisher.

Figure 14: from Viet, J., *EUDISED multilingual thesaurus for information processing in the field of education*, English version, Council of Europe and Mouton & Co., 1973. Reproduced by permission of the publishers.

Figure 15: from Viet, J., *Macrothesaurus for information processing in the field of economic and social development*, 3rd ed., UN, 1985, copyright United Nations and the Organisation for Economic Co-operation and Development (1985). Reproduced by permission.

Figure 16: from Aitchison, J., and others, *Thesaurofacet: a thesaurus and faceted classification for engineering and related subjects*, English Electric Co. Ltd, 1969. Reproduced by permission of GEC.

Figure 17: from Roberts, Michael J., and others, *Construction industry thesaurus*, 2nd ed., Property Services Agency, 1976. Reproduced with the permission of the Controller of HMSO, Crown copyright.

Figure 18: from the *ROOT thesaurus*, 2nd ed., British Standards Institution, 1985. Reproduced by permission of the publisher.

Figure 19: from the 'Art and architecture thesaurus' (AAT), The Getty Art History Information Programme, in progress. Reproduced by permission of AAT.

Figure 20: from Aitchison J., and others, *Thesaurus on youth: an integrated classification and thesaurus on youth affairs and related topics*, National Youth Bureau, 1981. Reproduced by permission of the publisher.

Figure 21: from Defriez, P., *The ISDD thesaurus: keywords relating to the non-medical use of drugs and drug dependence*, Institute for the Study of Drug Dependence, 1980. Reproduced by permission of the publisher, © Institute for the Study of Drug Dependence.

Figure 22: from Austin, D., *PRECIS: a manual of concept analysis and subject indexing*, 2nd ed., British Library, 1984. Reproduced by permission of the British Library Board.

Figure 24: from the *IRRD thesaurus*, 2nd ed., Organisation for Economic Co-operation and Development, 1985. Reproduced by permission of the publisher.

Figure 25: from Viet, J., and Van Slype, G., *EUDISED multilingual thesaurus for information processing in the field of education*, English version, Council of Europe, the Commission of the European Communities and Mouton & Co., 1984. Reproduced by permission of the publishers.

Figure 26: from BS 6723: *Guidelines for the establishment and development of multilingual thesauri*, BSI, 1985. This and the extracts from BS 5723: *Guidelines for the establishment and development of monolingual thesauri*, 2nd ed., BSI, 1987 are reproduced by permission of the British Standards Institution. Complete copies can be obtained from BSI at Linford Wood, Milton Keynes, MK14 6LE.

Figure 27: from Aitchison, J., 'Integrated thesaurus of the social sciences: design study', prepared for UNESCO Division for the International Development of the Social Sciences, UNESCO, 1981. Reproduced by permission of UNESCO.

Figure 28: from Niehoff, R.T., and Mack, G. *Final report on evaluation of the Vocabulary Switching Sytem*, Battelle Columbus Laboratories, 1984. Reproduced by permission of Battelle Memorial Institute.

Figure 29: from Knapp, S.D., Creating BRS/TERM, a vocabulary database for searchers, *DATABASE*, December 1984. Reproduced by permission of Online Inc.

Extracts of ISO 2788: *Guidelines for the establishment and development of monolingual thesauri*, 2nd ed., ISO, 1986 are reproduced with the permission of ISO – International Organization for Standardization, 1, rue de Varembé, 1211 Geneva 20, Switzerland.

Index